Praise for

"[Joann] shares such a variety of mindfulness experiences that we can explore this book for many seasons."

—Eric Imbody, qigong teacher, psychotherapist, and gardener

"If you are looking for fun ways to practice mindfulness, you will love *Growing Mindful*. Joann provides the reader with many wonderful and insightful games and activities to allow you to experience gardening, nature, and any other part of life in a more mindful way. I love how some of the activities allowed me experience my garden in new ways—with a level of awareness and clarity I had not experienced before. I highly recommend this book."

—Scott White, gardener and tai chi/qigong teacher

"The combination of horticultural information and Joann's personal stories will create a place for this book on many gardener's bookshelves. The way it guides one to a place of inner peace and deep appreciation for all that exists in the present moment earns it a place in the hearts of millions more seeking a path through these difficult times."

—Tracy Neal, landscape designer and teacher
through the Santa Fe Botanical Garden

Growing Mindful

© Jerrell Jones

About the Author

Joann Calabrese is a skilled wellness, mindfulness, and recovery educator. She is a lifelong organic gardener and herbalist, experienced in meditation, ritual work, qigong, and tai chi. Her passion is sharing how these intersecting practices can lead to more connectedness and healing in the world through workshops and coaching. Joann co-creates an urban backyard sanctuary for humans and other critters in Denver, Colorado, where she lives with her dog, Luna. She blogs at www.mindfulnessgardengames.com and posts on Instagram @mindfulnessgardengames.

GROWING MINDFUL

EXPLORATIONS in
the GARDEN to DEEPEN your
AWARENESS

JOANN CALABRESE

Llewellyn Publications
Woodbury, Minnesota

FIRST EDITION
First Printing, 2021

Book design by Samantha Peterson
Cover design by Shira Atakpu
Interior art on pages 45, 50, 51, and 52 by Llewellyn Art Department
Plant illustrations by Eugene Smith

Llewellyn Publications is a registered trademark of Llewellyn Worldwide Ltd.

Library of Congress Cataloging-in-Publication Data (Pending)
ISBN: 978-0-7387-6477-1

Llewellyn Worldwide Ltd. does not participate in, endorse, or have any authority or responsibility concerning private business transactions between our authors and the public.

All mail addressed to the author is forwarded but the publisher cannot, unless specifically instructed by the author, give out an address or phone number.

Any internet references contained in this work are current at publication time, but the publisher cannot guarantee that a specific location will continue to be maintained. Please refer to the publisher's website for links to authors' websites and other sources.

Llewellyn Publications
A Division of Llewellyn Worldwide Ltd.
2143 Wooddale Drive
Woodbury, MN 55125-2989
www.llewellyn.com

Printed in the United States of America

This book is dedicated to Samuel Copeland, whose wisdom, love, and support graced my life for too short a time. Your presence made the world a better place. You are missed.

Deep gratitude to family and friends who have been cheerleaders, advisers, proofreaders, and problem-solvers throughout this endeavor. I couldn't have done it without you.

Disclaimer

The information presented here is based on my relationship with plants. It is gleaned from my observations, experiences, the books I have read, and the garden lore passed down to me. None of my stories or experiences with plants should be taken as nutritional or medical advice. Consult with your healthcare practitioner or an herbalist before using or ingesting any plant or herbal product that you are unfamiliar with. Caution is advised when using or ingesting new plants or herbs, especially if you are prone to allergies.

CONTENTS

Part I
GREEN WORLD EXPLORATIONS

Part 2
PLANT CORRESPONDENCES AS MINDFUL FOCUS

INTRODUCTION

This book is a doorway to awareness of the flow of present moments. It does it in the most enjoyable way I know: through the garden and the green world. This is not a book about how to garden, but one of mindful explorations *in* the garden. Mindful explorations are activities that help us tune in to the present moment, using the garden as a portal.

It's funny how our minds conspire to take us any place but that flow. We try to nail things down with labels, replay the past, or envision the future. Often, just the act of being in a garden or in the natural world can help our brain calm down, allowing awareness to seep in. We intuitively sense how beneficial this is for us, as people naturally seek out parks, rivers, mountains, and other green spaces.

This book begins with the basic understanding that the green world facilitates focused attention. Then we take it a step further by providing the tools to work with the green world in a more active, direct way. The activities in this book are designed to help you open doorways to awareness on a more consistent basis.

When we are in the flow, moments open into infinity. Poets and philosophers have often described this state of waking up. While viewing a field of sunflowers, inhaling the fragrance of a rose, or planting a seed, something shifts. We become fully present to the immenseness of the universe, simultaneously understanding our small place in it and our relationship to all that is.

There are a host of books that detail the physical and emotional health benefits of mindfulness, but many try to despiritualize the practice. This strikes me as odd. If spirituality is tuning in to our connection to something greater than ourselves, then mindfulness is a spiritual practice. It's a remembrance of who and what we are.

Mindful practices facilitate deep awareness, gratitude, and understanding of our connectedness to all things. This is not simply an intellectual understanding, but instead a body-mind-spirit deep awareness.

Garden Connections

Life is a flowing river, not a series of static events. When we move into experiencing the flow, we are practicing mindfulness. Gardens and green spaces give us easy access to mindfulness practice. A garden, by its very nature, is a place of wonder and beauty. Gardens engage all our senses, helping us tap into the flow of moments. Plants are nonthreatening, so being in a garden provides a calm feeling of safety and openness that supports mindfulness practice.

Some of the earliest meditation and awareness masters have promoted the idea of meditating outdoors to be closer to the natural world while meditating. The Buddha sat under a Bodhi tree to reach enlightenment. Masters of tai chi and qigong (both movement meditations) often recommend practicing outdoors. When we are outdoors, we are closer to the natural energies that nurture and support us, creating a conducive environment for engaging with the flow.

Western science is catching up with what people have intuitively known: being in the natural world makes us feel good. Studies in the last few years show positive benefits to being outdoors.[1]

Most importantly, when we take the time to connect to the natural world, we realize that connection is there for us all the time. We simply need to stop and engage. As a culture, we have created boundaries to this knowingness, yet it seems so obvious when we look. Here we are, on this planet which supports us and provides everything we need, and yet, humans often seem oblivious to this vital support. By taking the time to stop and recognize our connections, we are enabling ourselves to make better judgments about the environment, our place in it, and the planet as a whole.

---

1. Robbins, "Ecopsychology."

What Is Mindfulness?

Language can help us understand the world, but it can also create confusion. The word *mindfulness* was first used by scholar T. W. Rhys Davids in 1910 as he worked to translate a Buddhist text written in the Pali language. Davids struggled to find the right English translation for the word *sati*, and he eventually settled on *mindfulness*.[2] There is no exact translation for this word, but it refers to awareness and remembrance, as in remembering who we really are in the present moment.

So, in some ways, the word mindfulness is a misnomer. We don't want our mind to be full; we are actually trying to quiet the busy mind, which is always comparing, analyzing, and traveling to the past and the future. Our goal during a mindfulness practice is to be aware of presence, the entire gestalt of existence, not just the words running through our heads.

This is the simple explanation for mindfulness that I use in workshops: "Mindfulness is bringing our awareness to the flow of present moments." This description captures the idea of movement and flow as well as our responsibility to focus our attention. It is an intentional activity.

The practice of paying attention via meditation (and other techniques) has been rooted in interactions with the natural world for thousands of years. Because this word and the recent interest in mindfulness blossomed from Buddhism, we often think this is the only place it existed, yet many spiritual traditions have contemplative practices that promote connectedness.

Connectedness

Experiencing connectedness is a benefit of mindfulness practice. Connectedness is the feeling and understanding of being part of a larger circle of energy and life on the planet. Most people have an intellectual understanding of connectedness. Connectedness is all around us if we take the time to look for it.

We know that the water circulating on the planet has taken a journey, flowing through rivers and nourishing people and plants and animals, flowing through us and then back to the clouds before being returned to rivers and oceans. Water has a cycle of connectedness, as do all of the elements.

---

2. Lomas, "Where Does the Word 'Mindfulness' Come From?"

We also know that sunlight enables plants to make food. Whether we eat plants or the animals that have eaten plants, we are being supported and connected by the sun, which bathes our planet with energy. This is a simple but powerful example of connectedness.

Science now confirms what energy healers and shamans have known for ages: fields of energy surround our bodies and can affect the energy fields of those around us.[3] We can affect others with our positive or negative energy in a very real way.

Everything on the planet is connected. Although we can work our way to this intellectual understanding of connectedness, experiencing connectedness is not a cerebral activity. It is a heart and body–centered energetic awareness. When connected, we experience the visible and invisible energies that touch us all, providing tangible support, nurturing, and wisdom.

There are personal benefits to experiencing connectedness, but I think there are global benefits as well. I think connectedness would help us solve many of the problems humanity faces. Having a strong sense of connection creates empathy and makes it more likely that a group will reach a consensus. It can bring about a collective understanding of a problem and how to solve it. If we, as humans, have a deep understanding that we are part of a larger organism, we might act differently. Mindful awareness helps provide a pathway to that understanding.

A Little About Me

I first began meditating in the early 1970s in an Edgar Cayce[4] study group, and I have maintained a consistent practice since then. I was raised Catholic and taught that wisdom was passed down in a hierarchal fashion, so it was a profound shift for me to sit in silence and tap into my internal wisdom. At that time, instruction and classes were hard to come by, so my friendship circle supported each other as we explored and learned to meditate, supplemented by workshops and cassette tape instruction. Our first intention was always to connect to our spiritual selves and divine nature.

---

3. McCraty, *The Energetic Heart.*

4. For more information on Edgar Cayce, see the Edgar Cayce's Assocation for Research and Enlightenment website, www.edgarcayce.org.

I think what we got wrong at the beginning was that we did not understand the holistic nature of meditation and mindfulness. We could sit in meditation for long periods of time and focus our thoughts, but we left our bodies and emotions behind. In our novice thinking, they were parts of ourselves to ignore or cast off.

The counterbalance to this was growing up in a gardening family. I had my hands in the soil from an early age and was aware—in a nonverbal, intuitive way—of my connection to the earth. For some reason, I considered the peace and contentment I felt while gardening to be totally separate from religion.

That all changed when I discovered an earth-centered spiritual path that was rooted in sensing the wonder and magic of being alive in our bodies and appreciating the communities on this planet. The green world and other nonhuman beings are counted in those communities. It's all connected.

Acknowledging and celebrating the sacredness of the earth was a shift in perception, but it wasn't the only shift I experienced. Our lives are tapestries with many threads woven into the fabric of who we are. Some of the other dominant threads of influence for me have been learning about healing plants, permaculture, my work in the nonprofit world, and ritual and energy work.

My love of gardening propelled me to learn more about healing herbs, in part because they were companion plants that helped vegetables grow. Delving into their histories and unique properties, I began to understand that the discovery of plants' healing properties had as much to do with intuition as observation. Early herbalism was an energy-sensing art as much as a science.

Then I discovered permaculture, a design system of sustainable practices. I had been an organic gardener for many years when I first watched a video about permaculture. While organic gardening is a set of practices centered around care of the soil and growing food without pesticides, permaculture takes a much broader view. Its overall goal is sustainability and increased food production, but the philosophy is about connectedness. That instantly got my attention.

I earned a permaculture design certificate many years ago, and although I never used my certificate professionally, my home and garden sanctuary reflect permaculture concepts. Perennials are interplanted with annuals, existing space and resources are used creatively, and I incorporate diverse plants. Permaculture also grabbed my attention because of its understanding that weedy plants like dandelion, nettle, and burdock have many benefits for the soil—and humans as well!

Permaculture has impacted the way I see the world as one interconnected organism. The guiding principles can be applied not only to the earth, but to human interaction as well. They have a spiritual perspective, which is not surprising because permaculture begins with connectedness. Some of the basic concepts include taking time to observe and understand a system, responding to change with creativity, and engaging in self-reflection. All of these are mindful practices for interacting with others on the planet and could be a playbook for intentional living.

Another influence in my life is the nonprofit world. With an undergraduate degree in social work and a master's degree in organizational leadership, I've spent much of my life in this realm. When functioning well, nonprofit organizations embrace a heart-centered path to bring positive change to the world. I've worked in various settings, but my current role is as a wellness and recovery educator. I provide training for individuals who will be assisting others with recovery from mental health conditions and substance use disorders. I also conduct workshops on mindfulness, trauma-informed practices, and wellness. Mindfulness practice guides me when dealing with challenging work situations, as does my work with plants. (The plant correspondences outlined in part 2 of this book provide continual insight on approaching problems with intentionality.)

One of the other threads in my life has been exploring modalities for sensing and working with energy. While living in Pennsylvania, I co-founded a women's ritual group and, with friends, created monthly full moon rituals. We created and nurtured group energy through meditation, drumming, chanting, and other focused activities. I also co-facilitated a drumming and chanting circle for over fourteen years and led Dances of Universal Peace, a kind of movement meditation that combines sacred dance and chant.[5]

Intentional movement is a way to bring us back into the here and now. Drum, dance, and chant are beautiful ways to increase group energy and cohesiveness, but I have found qigong to be a more direct path to sensing energy flow and cultivating increased awareness of presence. Qigong is a mind-body healing practice that originated in China.

I was introduced to qigong over twenty years ago through a deceptively easy form called the Eight Pieces of Brocade. It was my only daily qigong practice for many years. In 2002, I began a martial arts class that included tai chi. It

---

5. For more information, see the Dances of Universal Peace's website, www.dancesofuniversalpeacena.org/.

was taught by Grand Master Samuel Copeland, who this book is dedicated to. Tai chi is a martial art, but when executed slowly, it is also a mindful and healing practice, like qigong. Many instructors place tai chi under the umbrella of qigong.

To me, qigong is energy work, pure and simple. There are both stillness practices and movement practices within qigong, but even when we are still, we practice sensing the energy flow in and around our bodies. The flowing movements of qigong mimic the flow of energy in the natural world. Practicing in the garden, surrounded by living green entities, reinforces that awareness.

I incorporate qigong and tai chi movements into my workshops and also lead monthly mindfulness and qigong walks at Bluff Lake Nature Center in Denver, Colorado. In the last few years, I've completed my Practice Leader certifications with the Institute of Integral Qigong and Tai Chi (IIQTC) for both Level I Qigong and Tai Chi Easy.[6]

My life tapestry involves many different practices, all unified by spirituality and connectedness. Ultimately, all things come back to the garden for me. My work life is influenced by my time in the garden. Qigong is an extension of the flowing energies in the garden. There is wisdom to be gained in caring for plants and simply hanging out with them. They are allies, teachers, and healers on many different levels.

Mindfulness involves tuning in to the flow of life. Movement and non-movement are constantly morphing into each other. If we are paying attention, we can ride that wave. It's not complicated, but it requires practice and commitment to train your awareness. This book is an exploration of activities and rituals to do just that.

Jumping In: Helpful Tips and Tools

This book has two distinct parts. Part 1 is a kind of recipe book of green world mindfulness techniques and activities. Activities can be done in any order. You, the reader, can scan the topics and go where your intuition leads you. The activities are grouped into categories, but the practices don't always neatly fit into one category or another. Some of the activities are simple, fun attunements. Others might take a little more time to plan, and some require a commitment to practice

---

6. For more information, see the Institute of Integral Qigong and Tai Chi's website, www.instituteofintegralqigongandtaichi.org.

over time. Sampling the activities is a great way to get started, but repeating them will help deepen the practice. Repeating the same activity on a regular basis (daily or whatever your schedule allows) will open doorways to awareness.

Part 2 involves heart-centered and energetic explorations of garden correspondences. There is a long tradition with herbalists and alchemists of identifying plant correspondences. These are energetic characteristics of a plant, beyond their nutritional or medicinal traits. In this section, we'll work with one plant and its energetic correspondence for one week at a time. By planting that "seed" in your awareness, you can allow it to grow and focus your attention. There are fifty-two entries, making this ideal for a year's worth of practice, if you so choose.

You can begin anywhere, but it makes the most sense to read over the introductory sections for parts 1 and 2 before choosing activities. Both parts of the book can be used simultaneously or separately. You may be drawn to one part or another. That is okay—the parts are just different ways to approach green world mindfulness. Follow your intuition.

I've included the two-part botanical names for readers who may be interested. Botanists have worked out a naming system that helps ensure they are speaking about the same plant. The first part of the name is the genus, which identifies a group of plants with similar characteristics. The second part relates to the species of the plant and identifies its more specific features. The species name also differentiates it from others in its group. Most of the names are derived from Greek or Latin. Rest assured, it's not necessary to know botanical names when cultivating green world awareness.

Suggested Supplies

- A journal. This can be a simple spiral-bound notebook or another notebook of your choosing. It can be fun to pick out a special notebook for recording observations and experiences, and it can strengthen your commitment to practice.
- Writing tools. You'll need something to write and draw with. I suggest colored pencils for drawing and gel pens for writing. Colored pencils are affordable and provide a sensory treat as they tend to flow more easily on paper and create colorful recordings of our observations.

Gel pens are fun to write with and increase the likelihood that you will write in your journal.

- Access to a garden or other green space. You don't need your own garden to do these activities. Any green space where you are comfortable will work: a public park, a friend's backyard, a hiking trail, a public garden, an arboretum or conservatory, a patio garden, or next to your indoor houseplants.

Beginning Each Activity: Grounding and Centering

When beginning any of the explorations in either part of the book, take a few moments to ground and center yourself. Grounding is the letting go of excess energy so that you can be fully present. This excess energy might be a feeling of agitation, mental worries, or a preoccupation with something. An easy way to ground yourself is to take one to three intentional, deep breaths. On the exhales, feel or imagine any chaotic energy streaming out through your feet and fingertips and into the ground. This is a cleansing breath, allowing you to let go of what you don't need so you can focus on the activity.

To center yourself, take another deep breath or two and bring your attention to the core of your being. Mindfulness is a full-body experience, not an intellectual exercise. If your focus is still mostly in your head, place your hands on your diaphragm and feel it expanding and contracting as you breathe. Consciously move your attention from your head to your core.

These opening breaths can be done in a few minutes. Don't skip them. They help us shift into a focused mindfulness practice.

Endings: Closing with Intention

When ending an activity, even the very short ones, take a few moments to intentionally close. Reflect on the activity and what, if anything, you discovered. Most of the explorations in this book have suggested questions that you can answer in your journal. I have found journaling to be a great tool for allowing insights and feelings to percolate into my awareness. Just the act of putting pen to paper seems to unlock hidden knowledge and emotion. I might start by writing about something that is at a conscious level, and suddenly other insights are flooding onto the paper. Journaling is also a way to cultivate full-body awareness by writing about feelings and energetic discoveries after the activities. Capturing our discoveries in this way also provides a record of our mindfulness journey.

Many people have an aversion to writing because a teacher or someone else convinced them they couldn't write. Keeping a journal is not about writing essays that someone is going to grade. Recording discoveries in a journal is a focusing activity. It can include doodling, drawing, writing random words, or a combination of these things. Mostly importantly, the journal is *yours*. You don't have to share it with anyone. Misspelled words don't matter. I encourage you to give journaling a try.

There is, of course, the option to record insights electronically on a tablet, laptop, or even your phone. There are now options to write with a stylus on a tablet. I briefly tried journaling electronically and quickly returned to paper and pen. Experiment to find out what works best for you, but be aware that bringing any electronic device out to the garden might be more of a distraction than a help.

Gratitude for the Green World

As we approach any of these explorations, we want to remember that we are interacting with living beings. Each plant has a life force and a focus on living and thriving. Whenever we are harvesting plants, either part or all of the plant, we can take a moment to acknowledge the plant and its gift to us. Thanking the plant, silently or aloud, with intention is a good practice to adopt.

On Committing to Practice

This is a workbook. The activities are meant to be experienced. Mindfulness is a skill, and like playing the violin or creating art, one that gets better with practice. So just jump in and begin building your practice. You'll like some activities better than others. Stay with those, but also try out some others that you aren't immediately drawn to. They may surprise you.

Making a commitment goes a long way to warding off inertia. Decide how much time you will devote to your practice. Many of the activities in this book can be experienced in ten to fifteen minutes. Pick some activities that interest you and make a plan to stay engaged.

A caution: One way to sabotage your practice is to commit to more than you can do. Be realistic about what your available time is and set your goals accordingly. You can always do more! Set reasonable goals so that you can achieve success.

PART 1
GREEN WORLD
EXPLORATIONS

Green world explorations use the garden and natural world as a portal to deepening awareness. The activities fall into broad categories grouped by similarity. The categories are a way to organize the information, but some activities fit multiple categories. The categories are: sensory, movement, creative craft, culinary creation, elemental, deepening awareness, and contemplation.

Cultivating an attitude of curiosity and fun as we approach mindfulness keeps the explorations light and easy. There is nothing to fail at—we just do the practice. In a world of a million distractions, mindfulness is a challenging practice. But if we develop a playful approach, each time we lose focus, we can simply smile and begin again.

Green world mindfulness practice does not work as a thought experiment. It requires us to go outside and experience our connection to the natural world. Pick an exploration and try it. There are many choices here, and some will call to you more loudly than others. Try not to dismiss an activity you may have done before. Be willing to experiment and try it in a new way.

Within each category, activities will have the following information:

- Name of Exploration
- Type of Exploration
- Supplies Needed
- Ideal Setting
- Child Friendly: Yes or No

You can begin anywhere.

one

SENSORY EXPLORATIONS

We are often oblivious to what we are seeing, hearing, tasting, feeling, and smelling. We might halfheartedly sense something when we are occupied with another activity: we eat while we are driving; we interact with family members while texting. Yet our senses provide a direct connection to the flow of present moments, if we would only pay attention.

One of my earliest green world memories is running through the paths of my grandfather's garden. The tall staked tomatoes and corn created living tunnels for me and my siblings to run through. As we brushed against the plants, the tomatoes released their distinct fragrance and the corn stalks rattled in their raspy voices. It was a full sensory experience.

Sensory explorations are a good entry point for all of us, as they immediately connect us to the natural world.

Awareness of Sight

The explorations in this section help us engage with our sense of sight. The first three explorations work well together and can be done as a series of activities. Two of them involve drawing, but they are not about creating art; they are about seeing. The process of drawing helps us tune in to what is in front of us.

Choosing a Plant

You'll need a plant, or part of a plant, to work with for these activities. It can be a tree, a bush, or a smaller plant. When selecting a plant, I encourage you to walk around your green space and take time to look at plants as if you are seeing them for the first time. Pay attention to the shape, color, and texture. Ideally, select a plant that is calling to you in some way. You may also want to choose a plant based on the weather or your physical abilities.

Other considerations when choosing a plant:

- Are you comfortable standing or kneeling?
- Can you sit on the ground to observe a plant?
- Would you prefer to sit in a chair and have the plant be closer to eye level?

If it is not possible to stay outside to observe a plant for the entire activity because of weather, you can do this exercise with a houseplant or by bringing part of a plant indoors. And yes, these activities can be done in any season. Many plants lose their leaves in the winter, but there is much to observe on stems and branches.

Once you've identified your plant, you can begin.

Exploration
TUNING IN

Type of Exploration: Sensory (sight)

Supplies Needed:
- Journal or paper
- A flat surface to write on (such as a clipboard or large book)
- Pen or pencil

Ideal Setting: Outdoors with a favorite plant, but this can also be done indoors with a potted plant or part of a plant you've brought indoors

Child Friendly: Yes

Sit or stand in front of your plant and just observe. Ask yourself what you are seeing. Often our first response is to label the plant. We think, "I am looking at a cherry tree" or "This is a rose bush." Sometimes words get in our way and prevent us from seeing what is in front of our eyes. Let go of the names of the plants and instead use adjectives to describe what you see. Pretend you are a botanist from another planet seeing this plant for the first time and you are writing home about it.

- How would you describe it?
- What is your overall sense of the plant? (Healthy, vibrant, young, bright, energetic, etc.)
- What are the plant's colors?
- What shape is the whole plant?
- What shape are the plant's leaves?
- How do the stems attach to the plant?
- What do the plant's flowers look like? (If applicable)
- Does the plant creep along the ground, or does it cling to things and climb?
- Are parts of the plant sharp, soft, fuzzy, or angular?

Take your journal and write down every word or phrase that you can think of that represents this plant. You do not need to write in complete sentences; in some ways, trying to write full sentences might slow you down. Just identify what you are seeing and capture your words and thoughts on paper. This is an example of my writing on garden sage during winter:

full, bushy, grey, green, stem-y, strong, rooted, beautiful, distinct, soft, arrow-leaves, confident, powerful

Next, refocus your attention on a small part of the plant, one leaf, or a section of stem. How would you describe this small part of the plant? Many of your words might be the same, but not all of them should be. This is an example of my writing on one small leaf of garden sage during winter:

crinkled, soft, grey, small, curved, cave-like,
smooth, ridged edges, curling

Sit with the plant a little longer, just observing. When you are ready, record your thoughts in your journal. What did you discover? What surprised you?

Exploration
HAND TO PAPER #1

Type of Exploration: Sensory (sight)

Supplies Needed:
- Journal or paper
- A flat surface to write on (such as a clipboard or large book)
- Pen or colored pencils
- Tape

Ideal Setting: Outdoors with a favorite plant, but this can also be done indoors with a potted plant or part of a plant you've brought indoors

Child Friendly: Yes, recommended for ages six and up

The first thing to know about this activity is that it is not about making art. We are not looking for a finished product that is an accurate drawing or representation of what we are seeing. The goal is to focus your vision and really see the plant, often noticing things you've never seen before. Focusing on an object in this way can be a kind of meditation, to really see the object and all of the nuances, the color, the shape, the form. Let go of any judgment you have about your artistic skills. (Sometimes our drawings are quite interesting, but they are still not the point of this activity.)

I have, over many years of gardening, taken the time to do this activity with all my favorite plants. It is a way to connect and learn more about each plant. It sharpens my ability to pay attention and my appreciation for each plant's beauty and uniqueness. When I introduce this activity in mindfulness workshops, participants are often surprised by what they find when they tune in to a plant they thought they knew.

I am very partial to using colored pencils for my drawings because they create a soft impression of what I am trying to represent. I have found that markers can be too bold, and crayons are lovely but not very precise. Experiment to see what you prefer. You can also use any type of paper, but plain white sketching paper will work best and add to the experience. The pencils and paper you use don't have to be high quality, but if you can afford a step up from basic copy paper and the dollar store colored pencils, you'll notice a difference in the experience.

~~~~~~

Begin the exercise by simply being present to the plant in front of you. In the previous exploration, you made a list of all the descriptive words you associated with your plant. Now you will be tuning in to the twists, turns, and nuances of the shape of the plant. Focus on a part of the plant that interests you (stem, leaf, flower, etc.). You will not be able to draw the entire plant during this exercise.

It is helpful to tape your blank paper in place, whether to a table or other hard surface, so it does not move as you are drawing. Position yourself so you can easily see the plant. Place your pencil on the paper where you want to begin your drawing. Once you do that, you will not look at your paper for the rest of the activity. This will be challenging, but it will help you focus on what you are seeing. Remember: this is not about a finished product. This is a way to help your eyes focus on what is in front of them.

Looking only at the plant, begin to trace the form that the plant is taking with the pencil on the paper. Try to capture every small bump and turn. Do this for at least three minutes, focusing your eyes only on the plant.

Your finished drawing may look beautiful or comical. That's fine. Return your focus to the plant. Then record your insights in your journal. Did the activity help you see anything you missed when observing the plant's attributes? What unique features did you notice about the plant? What surprised you? What challenged you? What delighted you?

This activity might be difficult to explain to very young children. It should be possible to do with most children ages six and up. Because children can be very literal, you may want to avoid calling it a drawing activity. Emphasize that we are using pencil on paper to help us see better, which is exactly what we are doing.

Exploration
HAND TO PAPER #2

Type of Exploration: Sensory (sight)

Supplies Needed:
- Journal or paper
- A flat surface to write on (such as a clipboard or large book)
- Pen or colored pencils

Ideal Setting: Outdoors with a favorite plant, but this can also be done indoors with a potted plant or part of a plant you've brought indoors

Child Friendly: Yes, recommended for ages eight and up

This next activity follows a more familiar experience of drawing. The challenge with this is that most people feel they cannot draw and their self-judgment takes over. As with the last activity, you will have a representation of the plant on paper, but this exploration is not about the drawing. It is about focusing your eyes. Let go, if you can, of wanting the results to be artist quality.

Sit quietly and observe the plant again. If you've done the previous two activities, there are many features to tune in to. Find a place on the plant that you want to draw and start there. Continue drawing for at least five minutes to give yourself enough time to capture details of the plant: the curves, lines, notches, and bumps. Draw for longer than five minutes if it feels right. The goal is not to have a completed picture of the whole plant, but to have the part that you do complete be detailed with the features of the plant.

As in the previous activity, record your discoveries in your journal. Were you able to tune in to any additional, unique characteristics of the plant? What surprised you? What challenged you?

Exploration
SEEKING NEW AND DIFFERENT

Type of Exploration: Sensory (sight) and movement

Supplies Needed:

- A garden or green space where you can walk

- Journal or paper

- Pen or pencil

Ideal Setting: A green space you can get to easily, as this exploration involves repeat visits

Child Friendly: Yes

Begin with a conscious intention to notice changes and things that are new in your green space. It helps to state your intention before you begin to walk, such as: "I'm aware that each moment is new and different, and I am tuning in to the newness."

Before you begin walking, breathe in the energy of this green space and let your eyes take in the whole area. Then, as you begin to slowly walk through the garden, stop frequently and focus on individual plants. Notice their shape, color, and overall design. This activity is easiest to do in spring and summer when gardens are changing dramatically throughout the day. However, fall and winter provide an opportunity to pay more attention and hone our attentiveness and connection.

Record your observations in your journal. What discoveries did you make?

This is a great activity to do with children. It honors their need for movement and their natural curiosity. Try imagining you are explorers together.

Exploration
TREASURE HUNT

Type of Exploration: Sensory (sight) and movement

Supplies Needed:

- A magnifying glass would be useful, but is not necessary

Ideal Setting: A garden or green space where you can walk

Child Friendly: Yes

Opening your eyes and being aware of all that is happening in the garden has endless variations. Before you begin to walk through your garden or green space, set an intention for what you will be observing. Choose a treasure to focus on. This is a specific plant or green world feature to search for and be aware of. This will be limited only by your garden space and your imagination. Some suggested categories are:

- Flower buds that are just starting to open
- Flowers that are fading
- Seedpods
- Plants just emerging from the ground
- Bees
- Flying insects
- Crawling insects
- Insects on flowers
- Shapes in the garden (circles, ovals, spirals, etc.)
- Patterns in the garden (all the tall plants, all the small plants, shapes of leaves, etc.)
- Specific colors or variations of colors

If you are going to observe small features, try using a magnifying glass to enhance that ability.

This activity is perfect for children, and they might have great ideas for other categories. If you are doing this activity with children, remember that ideally, it is done silently. That gives everyone time to focus. Discussing what was discovered can be done after everyone has time to observe.

Although this is a great activity for children, don't assume it is not a deep practice. Focusing your attention on one category helps you stay present. You can appreciate subtle differences and changes in the garden.

I love this activity because it helps me attune to the smaller details in the garden. My yard has multiple beds and planting areas with many colors and shapes. When I take the time to search for specific shapes or insects, it focuses my attention. I practice this activity year round while going for walks. I search for buds forming on tree limbs and shrubs to notice the first visible signs of spring as they swell and prepare to open.

Exploration
BECOMING AN ALIEN

Type of Exploration: Sensory (sight)

Supplies Needed:
- Journal or paper
- Pen or pencil

Ideal Setting: Your garden or other green space

Child Friendly: Yes

Close your eyes for a few moments and imagine this scenario. You are an alien just visiting the planet for the first time. Everything you see is new. Open your eyes as you imagine stepping out of your spaceship into a place of vibrant color and energy.

How would you describe what you are seeing to others on your home planet? If you have no labels for plants and components in the garden, what might you say? Let go of what you think you should be seeing and describe what is in front of you. Here are some suggested concepts to consider in your journal:

- Describe the light and dark
- Describe the overall visual sensation
- Describe shapes
- Describe colors blending together on plants
- Describe how images flow together

Awareness of Scent

My dog Luna bursts out the back door each morning and runs the entire perimeter of the yard with her nose to the ground. Once she's checked out the edges, she continues running around the yard in a zigzag pattern following scents throughout the yard. We live in an urban neighborhood with cats, raccoons, skunks, moles, and other exciting night creatures that she can detect. A dog's sense of smell informs their world. Our human sense of smell will never be as strong as a dog's. However, we can take the time to cultivate this sense and its ability to connect us to our world.

Scents have the power to anchor us in calmness, wonder, and presence. One of my own experiences involving a transformational scent happened many years ago when my youngest daughter was twelve. We were camping at a festival in New York. I attended a women's healing ritual in the afternoon, where I was introduced to an essential oil blend called Sanctuary.[7] During the ritual, the facilitator placed a dab of Sanctuary oil on each participants' forehead. I resonated with it immediately. It was strong, earthy, and centering. The ritual was powerful and exactly what I needed at that time to address some chaos in my life. The scent anchored the feeling of calmness and empowerment.

Later in the evening, someone came to my tent to tell me my daughter had dislocated her knee. She had been at the pool with friends and it popped out of place. This happened several times when she was twelve; without any provocation, her knee would dislocate. As I ran to the pool, I was immediately aware of the Sanctuary oil. The scent had stayed with me all day. Rather than my usual stressed reaction, I felt calm and ready to deal with a challenging situation. A nurse on-site at the campground tried to guide my daughter's knee into place without success, so I drove her to the emergency room, located an hour from the campground. I borrowed a friend's station wagon so she could stretch her leg out in the back as I drove.

Driving unfamiliar country roads in the dark with a child crying in the backseat is not a recipe for calm and centered emotions. However, that was exactly how I felt! The Sanctuary fragrance was helping me tap into serenity and peace. Ten minutes before we got to the emergency room, my daughter's

---

7. Sanctuary Oil is made by Sue-Ryn Hildenbrand-Burns of Hill Woman Productions in Wellesley Island, New York. Visit her website www.hillwoman.com to learn more.

knee popped back into place on its own, something that also frequently happened. While I was relieved that it had popped into place, I knew we still had to have her checked out.

Entering into a room with blazing fluorescent lights and emergency room noise was jarring, but I was again helped by the Sanctuary oil, which anchored me to centeredness. I often think of that night when I think of the power of smell in helping us be present and calm.

As with other senses, when we take the time to tune in to our sense of smell, it opens the door to the flow of present moments. Molecules of scents from the world are interacting with the nerve endings in our nasal passage to provide information and delight. If you are a gardener, you probably already tune in to garden fragrances on a regular basis. The following exploration activities offer ways to go deeper and notice the nuances.

Exploration
TUNING IN TO GARDEN SCENTS

Type of Exploration: Sensory (smell)

Supplies Needed:
- Journal or paper
- Pen or pencil

Ideal Setting: A garden or other green space

Child Friendly: Yes

Sit or stand in your garden or green space. You may want to close your eyes, which will allow you to focus more on your sense of smell. Inhale deeply through your nose. Stating an intention is also helpful: "I am open to connecting with the fragrances of this garden and green space. I am attentive to all the scents emanating from this green space."

Breathe in the energy of the green space and ask yourself what you are smelling. Unless you are close to one overpowering plant, there will probably be a mixture of smells, many of them very subtle. Give yourself enough time to settle in, focusing on your nose.

In your journal, write down every word or phrase you can think of that represents the overall fragrance of the garden. This does not have to be written in complete sentences and the words do not have to be words we traditionally associate with smell. Colors, animals, shapes, songs, or poems might present themselves. The idea is to capture your experience with this sense in your garden.

Here is an example of my writing using the sense of smell in my own garden on a spring morning:

freshness—openness—sparkly—wet—shimmering—vibrant—
sweet—jasmine—newness—emerald green

Continue to take in the fragrance of this space. Add any other insights and discoveries to your journal entry.

Exploration
GOING DEEPER WITH SCENTS

Type of Exploration: Sensory (smell) and movement

Supplies Needed:
- Journal or paper
- Pen or colored pencils

Ideal Setting: A garden or green space to walk in

Child Friendly: Yes, but watch for bees and plants with thorns, especially if exploring with younger children

In a garden, we may be overpowered by one or two strong fragrances and unable to tune in to the more subtle ones. Some plants have heavy fragrances that carry on the wind, making it hard to detect others. In the spring, my entire neighborhood carries the perfume of lilacs because they are so prolific. That's lovely, but it also makes it difficult to be perceptive of anything else.

What we want to do in this activity is move beyond this strong surface level of smells. As you did in the activity on listening, just sit or stand quietly for a few minutes and focus on what fragrances you are taking in as you inhale. Being outdoors has a different fragrance than being indoors. Be with that. If you live in a city or on a busy street, there may be scents that have nothing to do with a garden or green space, and yet here they are. The practice of being present means taking those scents in as well and just noting your dislike. Let go of judgment for the most part. Use common sense. If smells are toxic or there is an air pollution alert, it may be best to stay inside that day.

This activity differs from the previous one in that we begin to move slowly through the garden and put our nose close to flowering plants and inhale. (Watch for bees or other pollinators as you are doing this.) Many flowers have a light fragrance that is only noticeable when we get close. Flowers have a wide variety of fragrances, all with the intention of calling pollinators to them. There is a whole spectrum of smells; some we will love and others, not so much. I happen to love the musky fragrance of clary sage and the slightly acrid tinge of marigolds. Many people do not. There are ornamental pear trees planted in my son's neighborhood that give off a strong scent for a few days every spring that I find disagreeable. But the trees are gorgeous, and the smell is part of who they are. This activity is not about liking and disliking, although we can note those responses. It is about tuning in to plants, their personalities, and their vibrations.

Like getting to know something new about a friend, taking the time to tune in to smells connects us more deeply to these plants. Walk slowly through your garden or green space and lean in to smell the flowers of different plants.

Leaves and stems also have fragrances, especially the leaves and stems of culinary and medicinal herbs. Usually we need to brush against a plant to release the scent. For this part of the activity, make sure the plant you are brushing up against is not an allergen for you and does not have thorns, tiny hairs, or stinging parts. You can also use gloves to do this activity. If you don't have your own garden space and are using a public garden space, touching is usually allowed as long as you are not damaging the plants in any way. Just be conscious of that as you walk.

Try this activity at different times of the day. Some plants depend on night pollinators and do not release their fragrance until evening. The fragrance of nicotiana, for example, is imperceptible by day. At night, as the plant is calling out to evening pollinators, it has a strong jasmine-like smell.

When you've finished your garden walk, capture your experience and discoveries in your journal.

Exploration
CREATING A FRAGRANCE GAME

Type of Exploration: Sensory (smell)

Supplies Needed:

- Scissors
- Small containers (jelly jars, baby food jars, cups, etc.)
- A tray for setting the containers on (optional)
- Journal or paper
- Pen or pencil
- Tape

Ideal Setting: A garden or other green space where you have permission to snip parts of plants

Child Friendly: Yes

We can create a scent awareness game for ourselves or to share with others. This one is especially fun with children. The distinct fragrance of culinary herbs is a good place to start. Clip leaves of lavender, dill, basil, rosemary, summer savory, lemon balm, mint, or similar plants. As you clip each one, express gratitude to the plant for sharing its fragrance with you. Rub the leaves to release the fragrance and place each snippet of plant in its own small container. Write the name on tape and affix to the bottom of the jar. Wash your hands in between plants so the fragrances don't mix. Try this with six to ten plants to start. If you are doing this with small children, start with four or so.

Once the plant snippets are in jars, wash your hands thoroughly so you don't have any herbal fragrance on your hands when you begin. Find a place to sit quietly and lift each jar to your nose to breathe in the fragrance. Ideally, this should be done with eyes closed. Another option is to have the top of the container covered with a tissue so that there are no visual clues. Breathe in each plant and see if you can identify it by smell alone.

All plants and leaves have fragrances, but many are subtle. As you refine your sense of smell, you can tune in to lighter fragrances. Using snippets of vegetable leaves like tomatoes, beans, okra, and arugula (and weedy plants you may be pulling up anyway like dandelion, ground ivy, bindweed, and burdock) will make a more challenging game. You can also repeat the game with flowers.

This is a fun activity for children. They can help set up the game by choosing herbs and plants along with you. What child does not like tiny containers and games of smell?

Record in your journal any insights and discoveries.

Exploration
CREATING A FRAGRANCE GARDEN

Type of Exploration: Sensory (smell)

Supplies Needed:
- Planters
- Potting soil
- Seeds or cuttings from a friend's garden

Ideal Setting: A garden plot or near potted plants, whether they are on a patio or indoors

Child Friendly: Yes

Creating a fragrance garden is a long-term project, not unlike setting up a meditation area in your home. It may be something you want to consider. Planting fragrant herbs along a walkway where you will brush against them as you walk by can remind you to be present. You can also choose one area of the yard or garden to be a focal point for fragrance.

You can research plants that do well in your area or talk with someone at a local garden center to decide what you'd like to plant. Some common and easy-to-grow herbs include lavender, rosemary, sage, thyme, basil, mint, and lemon balm. Be aware that mint and lemon balm will spread rapidly, so you may want to sequester them in large pots or their own beds.

There are many fragrant flowers as well, but the advantage to growing fragrant herbs is that the perfume is in the leaves and will be around for the entire season. Some plants, like sage and lavender, hold on to their fragrance throughout the winter as well.

Apartment dwellers can also create a fragrant indoor garden with potted plants. Rosemary, thyme, and basil all do well in sunny window locations.

Once you've established which plants you want to pot, the key part of this activity is allowing the fragrance to be a reminder of mindfulness. Like the ringing of temple bells calling everyone back to the here and now, we can make a commitment to practice mindful awareness whenever we brush against the plants and release their fragrance.

I recommend using your journal to record ongoing observations with this practice.

Exploration
CAPTURING FRAGRANCES

Type of Exploration: Sensory (smell)

Supplies Needed:
- Garden herbs
- Scissors
- Garden twine
- Small squares of cotton fabric
- Ribbon

Ideal Setting: A garden or green space where you have permission to collect herbs

Child Friendly: Yes

Many culinary and medicinal herbs hold on to their fragrance for a long time. Finding ways to include these sweet-smelling plants in our lives can reduce stress and help us practice attuning to the present. There are many essential oils that capture the fragrance of plants. Creating essential oils requires some expensive equipment and many plants, but anyone can capture scents in an accessible and straightforward way by drying them.

Some of my favorite plants to dry are lavender, basil, sage, clary sage, rosemary, and thyme. You can look up the requirements for specific plants, but a basic procedure for drying herbs is as follows:

- Remember to thank the herb that you are using before you start to cut.

- Clip small bundles of herbs early in the morning after any dew has dried.

- Tie the stems and hang them upside down in a cool, dry place for a few days until they are completely dry. Drying time will vary depending on your location. Alternatively, the herbs can be laid out on a tray in a cool, dry place.

- Once completely dry, package the herbs into glass jars. Canning jars work well.

The herbs I suggested can be used for tea and to flavor your food. They can also be made into small herbal charms to keep nearby. Use a four to five–inch square swatch of cotton fabric. Place a generous amount of dried herbs in the center of the swatch. Bring the four corners together and tie them with a ribbon. Instantly, you have an herbal charm to take with you or to keep on your desk or dashboard. Squeezing the charm lightly will release the fragrance and remind you to practice awareness.

Awareness of Sound

The first time I visited Rocky Mountain National Park with my family, we hiked through a grove of aspen that looked just like I'd always imagined a fairy forest would look. The slight cream-colored trunks, mottled with grey, held branches of shimmering light-green leaves. The sight was beautiful, but it was the sound of the leaves gently rustling that completed the magic. Like thousands of papery windchimes, they created an enchanting soundscape. As other hikers rounded the path, there were notable gasps of awe. The composite of sight and sound was all encompassing.

Our gardens may not offer such an over-the-top experience, but that can be a good thing as we can stretch to sharpen our awareness of this sense. Seeing and smelling might seem like the easiest senses to tune in to in a garden. Focusing on sounds requires a little more attention. As a start, put away the earbuds and headphones for a while, and tune in to the space around you.

Exploration
TUNING IN TO THE GARDEN SOUNDSCAPE

Type of Exploration: Sensory (hearing)

Supplies Needed:
- Journal or paper
- Pen or pencil

Ideal Setting: A garden or other green space

Child Friendly: Yes

Sit or stand quietly in the garden and begin to pay attention to the sounds you are hearing. It may help to do this with eyes closed, if you are comfortable with that. It is also helpful to state an intention: "I am open to connecting to this garden/green space through sound. I am attentive to hearing all the sounds emanating from this green space."

First pay attention to the most obvious sounds you hear. Some may be in your garden and others might be sounds enveloping your garden. You may hear leaves rustling, prayer flags flapping, the buzz of bees, or hummingbird wings. You might also hear a neighbor's lawn mower, a dog barking, or conversations happening elsewhere. Notice those sounds and accept them as part of this soundscape. Don't push anything away. Just meet the sounds with curiosity and without labeling. I live in a cityscape, so neighborhood sounds are part of my garden sounds.

As you sit, allow sounds to wash over you. Become an open and receptive receiver of sounds, great and small. As you settle into listening, focus your attention on quieter and more subtle sounds. What sounds have been below your conscious awareness? What is the space between the sounds?

Give yourself some time to experience this activity. It's easy to walk away after a few minutes. Challenge yourself to notice the subtle sounds and silence. Sit for a minimum of ten minutes. See what you discover, then record it in your journal.

Exploration
GOING DEEPER WITH GARDEN SOUNDSCAPES

Type of Exploration: Sensory (hearing)

Supplies Needed:
- Journal or paper
- Pen or pencil

Ideal Setting: A garden or other green space

Child Friendly: Yes, although very young children might get impatient

This activity is an extension of the previous one. Pick a subtle sound to focus on. This could be leaves or corn stalks rustling, bees buzzing, or hummingbird wings flapping. It will be helpful to sit close to these happenings. For example, sit near a tree or close to flowers where bees are pollinating. In the summer, my garden buzzes with pollinators, but if you don't have a lot of flowers in your green space, you may have to visit a place that does.

Tune in to your chosen sound. It might ebb and flow or it might be a steady sound. If it ebbs and flows, be aware of the emptiness between sounds.

As in the last activity, let the sound wash over you. Become a receiver for this sound. It can act as a mantra, helping with focus and single-pointed awareness.

Consider how the sound is happening. When we hear rustling leaves, they are rubbing against each other, moved by air currents. Air currents are created by the sun, our burning star, as it heats the atmosphere. Currents form with warmer air rising and cooler air sinking. Air begins to flow and moves the leaves. The leaves touching each other cause vibration in the air, traveling to our ears and our brains. It's a magical process. Whether it is leaves, hummingbird wings, or our neighbor's dog barking, the process of hearing is equally amazing. As with the last activity, stay with this exploration long enough to settle in and allow discoveries to happen.

Record your experience in your journal.

Exploration
CREATING RHYTHM

Type of Exploration: Sensory (hearing)

Supplies Needed:
- Journal or paper
- Pen or pencil
- Small drum or flat surface that can be used as a makeshift drum (optional)

Ideal Setting: A garden or other green space

Child Friendly: Yes, for children old enough to discern rhythm

This activity involves creating a rhythm along with nature sounds. As a hand drummer, I tend to hear rhythms where none were intended. I've found it enlightening to sit in the garden with my eyes closed and let a rhythm present itself to me. I am open to the idea that rhythms are happening in any space—I simply need to turn my awareness to them. It is interesting to sit quietly and allow the disparate sounds to reveal themselves as a rhythm.

Drumming on your thighs is an easy and accessible way to do this. You can also use a small drum or any flat surface that can serve as a drum, like the arm of a lawn chair or the side of a planter. If using an actual drum, tap out the rhythm quietly so you don't overpower the sounds in your green space.

Begin by being still and tuning in to the sounds in your garden. Give yourself enough time to shift into a comfortable awareness of the sounds. It may be helpful to state an intention: "I am open to co-creating a rhythm with the sounds in this garden."

Listen with the intention of finding a rhythmical pattern. Making patterns out of stimuli is something we do quite naturally as humans, often with visual patterns, but we can do it with sound as well. When you feel like you have a rhythm to match the sounds, begin to tap it out softly on your thighs or makeshift drum. There is no right or wrong here. Whatever you create will be perfect in this moment, a co-creation with existing soundscape. It is not as much about the rhythm created as it is about the rhythm you are tuning in to.

Stop periodically to listen to just the sounds created by the green space and adjust your rhythm if you want to. This is an interesting activity to do with children as they may tune in to completely different sounds. Stay with this for a while; it is a subtle and profound way to listen deeply.

Record insights and discoveries in your journal.

Awareness of Touch

The soft, downy leaves of the ornamental lamb's ear plant are a favorite with my grandchildren. They love touching the plant, picking the leaves, and rubbing them against their faces to feel the soothing silkiness. As infants and children, we are all about exploring the world through touch. As we get older, we are more cautious, and although that's not a bad thing, it sometimes limits our interactions with the natural world.

Smooth, soft, rough, prickly, bumpy, scratchy—there are hundreds of ways a plant can feel to our touch. Taking the time to be familiar with the texture of plants is another way to be present and get to know each plant. Even gardeners may not have a familiarity with plant textures if they routinely wear gardening gloves.

A caution: Some plants can cause dermatitis or an allergic reaction, which is one of the reasons some gardeners wear gloves. In the two activities in this section, use plants that you are familiar with, look them up, or touch them cautiously at first. The plants included here are generally safe, but every person is different, so pay attention to any reactions you may have.

Exploration
TUNING IN TO TOUCH

Type of Exploration: Sensory (touch)

Supplies Needed:
- Journal or paper
- Pen or pencil

Ideal Setting: A garden or green space

Child Friendly: Maybe. Adults should explore the area first and supervise children if there are plants in the area that they should not touch. Some plants are scratchy and would be fine for adults to explore, but not small children.

This activity is about exploring the garden through touch. Some plants can cause dermatitis and other allergic reactions. Take some time to make a positive identification of a plant before touching. If you are new to gardening, get the input of an experienced gardener, a plant identification book, or both.

~~~~~~~~

As with the other senses, it can be good form to begin with an intention. "I am open to tuning in to tactile awareness in this garden. I am open to learning more about this green space through touch."

Begin to walk slowly through the garden and gently run your hands across plant leaves, flowers, stems, and branches that you are familiar with. Use your eyes to observe what parts are safe to explore. For example, it is fine to touch rose petals and leaves, but the stems have thorns. As an adult, you may want to gently explore the thorny stems, but this is not recommended for children. Similarly, raspberry leaves are textured and interesting, but raspberry stems are quite scratchy, and you may want to avoid them. If you are growing any type of hot pepper, don't handle the peppers with your bare hands, as they will burn. Also watch for bees and other pollinators.

Plants that are generally benign to touch include: marigold, calendula, dandelion, lemon balm, parsley, chamomile, fennel, mint, and most leafy greens. Dinosaur kale is especially interesting because of its bumpy texture.

Don't rush. Allow the tactile awareness to sink in. Exploring the tactile nature of plants is a matter of paying attention. Plants will surprise you; visually, you may expect one sensation and find the opposite when you touch the plant. Take your time and explore.

Record observations and discoveries in your journal. What, if anything, surprised you?

Exploration
CREATING A GAME OF TACTILE AWARENESS

Type of Exploration: Sensory (touch)

Supplies Needed:
- Scissors
- Small containers (jelly jars, baby food jars, cups, etc.)
- A tray to set the cups on (optional)
- Masking tape
- Journal or paper
- Pen or pencil

Ideal Setting: A garden or other green space where you have permission to snip parts of plants

Child Friendly: Yes, if the adults have made sure the plants are safe to touch

You can create a tactile awareness game for yourself or others. This is similar to the fragrance game in the Awareness of Scent section. The idea is to challenge yourself to identify plants by touch alone.

To begin, choose the leaves of plants that are safe to touch and have different textures to them: rough, smooth, feathery, soft, bumpy, mildly scratchy, etc. Avoid plants that are common allergens. Leaves to start with might include lamb's ear, rose, fennel, kale, cosmos, dandelion, marigold, chard, and lady's mantle. These are plant favorites in my garden. You can choose your own as long as they are safe to touch.

As you are clipping leaves off of your chosen plants, remember to thank them. Place each leaf in a small container and write identification on the bottom of the container. Begin with six to ten plants to start. Once the cuttings are in the jars, sit quietly and close your eyes. Pick up one plant cutting at a time and allow yourself—with eyes closed—to explore the feel of the plant, the nuances, dips, valleys, and bumps. Try to identify the plants by touch alone.

You can also repeat this with flowers from different plants: nasturtiums, cosmos, marigolds, dandelions, roses, lilies, etc. This may be an easier activity because you'll be relying on shape as well as texture.

Record observations in your journal. How hard or easy was it for you to identify plants by touch? What did you discover?

Awareness of Taste

My garden is a grazing garden. I've been intentional about including fruits and vegetables that are easy to pop into my mouth as I'm wandering about. My grandchildren love being able to nibble on plants as they move about the garden. In spring there are leaves of young dandelion, overwintering kale, violets, and chives, followed by strawberries and peas. By summer there are raspberries, currants, goji berries, cherry tomatoes, nasturtium, borage, and other edible flowers.

Mindfulness when tasting food involves surrendering to that sense to fully experience the flavor. We can of course practice this with fruits and vegetables we've purchased, washed, and prepared in some way. However, tasting a raspberry or tomato moments after it has been picked connects us to that plant immediately, and this is a great way to appreciate a garden.

Exploration
TUNING IN TO FLAVOR AND TASTE

Type of Exploration: Sensory (taste)

Supplies Needed:
- Journal or paper
- Pen or pencil

Ideal Setting: Your own garden or a garden where you have permission to pick and taste plants

Child Friendly: Yes, with adult supervision

This activity involves expanding our awareness of the flavors in our garden and green world. Because it involves ingesting plants, I caution you to start with common fruits and vegetables you know are safe to eat.

If you have your own garden, you might feel that you are already well-versed in its flavors, but you can always go deeper. Begin by attuning yourself to the garden space. Take some slow deep breaths. It is helpful to begin with an intention: "I am open to tuning in to taste awareness in this garden. I am open to learning more about this green space through flavor and taste."

Your choice of available plants may be limited by the seasons. Look around the garden and decide what plant you'd like to sample. Choose something small that will be easy to put in your mouth. As you pick the fruit or vegetable, thank the plant for providing sustenance.

Before placing it in your mouth, stop and consider this unique moment. A plant growing in the earth, nurtured by your energies, supported by the soil, water, air, and sun, is now ready to taste. Appreciate the moment and be fully present as you place it in your mouth. Notice the texture and weight on your tongue before you begin to chew. There might be only a slight flavor before you begin to chew. Tune in to that flavor. Then slowly begin to chew the plant, releasing the flavor into your mouth. Allow yourself to be fully immersed in the flavor as if experiencing it for the first time. Does the flavor change as you chew? Does the flavor stay in your mouth after you've swallowed? How would you describe it? Is it sweet, bitter, tangy, juicy, tart?

Record any insights in your journal.

Exploration
GOING DEEPER WITH FLAVOR AND TASTE

Type of Exploration: Sensory (taste)

Supplies Needed:
- Journal or paper
- Pen or pencil

Ideal Setting: Your own garden or a garden where you have permission to pick and taste plants

Child Friendly: Yes, with adult supervision

This activity is an expansion of the previous activity. It is a way to branch out and explore the taste of plants we've never considered before and maybe didn't even know were edible. Many common weeds and garden flowers are edible. This does require some research on your part to make sure the plant you are tasting is nontoxic. Be sure you have a positive identification for any plants you are tasting. You can also enlist the help of an experienced gardener.

~~~~~~~~~

While doing this activity, let go of what you think plants should taste like or the idea that you must enjoy everything you taste. Once you've confirmed that a plant is safe, allow yourself to experience its unique flavor in a nonjudgmental way.

I have a goumi (*Elaeagnus multiflora*) bush in my yard. It produces beautiful golden berries that turn bright red when ripe. The berries are edible, but they are not my favorite. They are very astringent and have an aftertaste that leaves my tongue feeling fuzzy. There is also a large seed in each berry, so there is not much fruit to enjoy. I leave most of the berries for wildlife, but eating a few berries is a way for me to appreciate and connect with the plant. This idea can be adopted for any edible plants in our green space.

Some common edible flowers are borage, calendula, lavender, nasturtium, hollyhock, clover, and day lilies (NOT Asiatic lilies). Common edible weeds include dandelion, burdock, shepherd's purse, lamb's quarter, clover, and chickweed. The young leaves of these plants are usually tastier. Many plants get bitter and harder to chew as they mature.

Once you have identified a plant you'd like to try, proceed as you did in the previous activity. Begin with an intention and be intentional as you taste and experience the plant.

Record discoveries in your journal.

Reflecting on Sensory Exploration

Engaging our senses in the garden is a fun and beautiful way to develop and strengthen our mindfulness practice. Gardens almost automatically invite sensory awareness. We can challenge ourselves to go deeper. Fully tuning in to our senses opens the door to greater connection to each moment and to the infinite. It's a matter of stopping and being present. When we are present, our senses will gift us with a connection to our flow.

two

MOVEMENT EXPLORATIONS

When I was first introduced to meditation and mindfulness, I did not understand that mindfulness can take many active forms. My first discovery of meditation in action was when I found chanting, the singing repetition of a sacred phrase. Drumming and dancing as movement meditation also became part of my practice at that time. It was a revelation to take some of what I had learned in a sitting meditation practice and to use it in focused activity and movement. In retrospect, it seems like the most logical thing in the world. Meditation and mindfulness should help us be more engaged in our daily activities. A focused movement practice is one way to develop the skills that we can move into our day-to-day lives. Practicing in a garden provides the additional bonus of easily engaging our senses.

Exploration
WALKING WITH BEAUTY

Type of Exploration: Movement

Supplies Needed:
- Journal or paper
- Pen or pencil

Ideal Setting: An outdoor space where you feel comfortable moving around

Child Friendly: Yes

Walking meditations are part of many traditional contemplative paths. To walk silently and be present with each step is both easier and more difficult than sitting meditation. It is easier because we like to be busy, so the movement helps keep us engaged. That is why this is an excellent exploration to do with young people. It's also great for adults who struggle to be still. This exploration can also be more difficult because we are moving, we can be more easily distracted from our task. Walking through our own garden presents other challenges. We may find ourselves making mental notes about what chores we need to do later rather than being present to what we are seeing and sensing. We also may find ourselves simply drifting away into some other activity. It is good to have a clear path and a prescribed way to walk.

Walking practice can be as simple or as complicated as we want to make it. A simple walking meditation involves walking through the garden or other green space and being as fully present as we can be. There are ways to structure this activity to help us along. This one is about recognizing beauty.

~~~~~~~

Begin by simply standing in the garden and being conscious of this space. Take as much time as you need. When you begin to take a first step, make sure it is a conscious choice. The goal is to be present in the garden and with your body. Pay attention to the way your body is moving in the garden, aware of each step on the path and each breath as you walk.

As you walk, synchronize your steps and breath. Use the rhythm of your breath. Your footsteps are the anchor. If you are new to the practice, stay with that synchronization for as long as you like (days, weeks, or longer). When you are ready, add a reminder phrase, like one of the following. (You can also make up your own phrases that carry meaning for you.)

- "I am walking in the garden. I am immersed in beauty."
- "I am absorbing the beauty of this garden on every level of my being."

- "I breathe in beauty. I release negativity to the healing earth."
- "I am breathing in the beauty all around me. I am releasing worries and fears."

When you come to the end of your walk, remain quiet for a little while and be in touch with sensations and experiences in your body.

Record your experience in your journal. How was it? What did you discover? What were you aware of?

Exploration
WALKING WITH EARTH ENERGIES

Type of Exploration: Movement

Supplies Needed:
- Journal or paper
- Pen or pencil

Ideal Setting: An outdoor space where you feel comfortable moving around

Child Friendly: Yes, recommended for ages eight and up

This activity is a walking practice based on energy awareness. We are practicing sensing the energy of the earth. It can be done with or without shoes. If you are comfortable barefoot, go for it! If not, the energy is still available for you to feel.

Stand in the garden and be present. Settle into your breathing, taking deep, full breaths. With each exhale, feel your breath sinking through your body and relaxing all your muscles. Let your shoulders relax and drop. At the same time, imagine yourself as a marionette with a string attached to the top of your head. Feel the string pulling your head up gently.

Know that the ground is supporting you and the planet is holding you close. Here you are on this planet, and the weight of your being is being supported by the earth. Bring your awareness to your feet. Feel the connection to the planet through your feet. If you cannot feel an actual connection, then imagine it. Gravity is holding you firmly in place. Take three to five deep breaths and become grounded in this connection.

Consciously think about the foot that you want to move first. Imagine or feel heaviness from the foot you are about to move flowing to the foot that will remain on the ground. Feel your movement foot becoming lighter and the foot remaining on the ground becoming heavier. Feel the grounded foot take on the full weight of your body and as you do, begin to lift your other foot. Sense the pull of gravity as you lift your foot. Lift it slowly up off the ground, paying careful attention to the balance needed to do this and the connection your weighted foot has to the ground. Slowly and with attention, step forward and place your moving foot on the ground. As it touches down, pay attention to the moment it touches the ground and the point on your foot where the connection was made. As you move, be aware of the earth's energy and the shifting weight in your body.

Be still for a moment. Then slowly begin to transfer all of the weight into the foot that just stepped down. Feel its connection to the earth and its heaviness. Once your weight is transferred, let your other foot come up off the ground. Do this consciously again: make the intention to move your foot, then consciously use your muscles and tendons to move your foot slowly off the ground. As before, slowly move your foot forward through space until you set it on the ground in front of you.

Continue to walk in this manner for as long as you like. Begin in small increments. Even taking ten steps while practicing full attention can be profound. This activity is not about getting somewhere quickly, but instead about tuning in as you move.

You probably have not thought this much about walking since you were a small child and you were just learning to walk. Walking is a complex process that we take for granted. We've learned to attune to gravity, balance, and the intricacies of our bodies, so we no longer give it our attention.

As you become comfortable with walking in this attentive way, you can begin to shift your awareness from the ground beneath your feet to the atmosphere and collective energies of the earth. Use the area around you to push the awareness even further. Observe the green space around you and feel the air on your face and skin. If there are plants within reach, touch them and make that connection as well. Feel or imagine yourself fading into the background to become simply one more energetic being in this green space. We are not isolated entities; we are part of a web of connectedness and movement. The ultimate goal of this exploration is to sense your connectedness with a green space and all of its aliveness and movement, even for just a few moments at a time.

Record any discoveries in your journal.

Exploration
LABYRINTH WALKING

Type of Exploration: Movement

Supplies Needed:
- An existing outdoor labyrinth or the materials and instructions to create your own[8]

Ideal Setting: An outdoor labyrinth

Child Friendly: Yes

The words *labyrinth* and *maze* are sometimes used interchangeably. However, the definitions have changed over time and there is a difference. A labyrinth is a path of many twists and turns that has only one way to proceed, unlike a maze, which has many false paths.

If you have a large garden space, you can set up a labyrinth close to your garden or through your garden. There are a number of traditional labyrinth patterns. One of the most famous appears in the Chartres Cathedral in France.

---

8. The Labyrinth Society has information on their website about how to construct a labyrinth. They also provide locations of public labyrinths. Read more at www.labyrinthsociety.org.

If you do not have the space, materials, or interest to create your own labyrinth, many cities have public outdoor labyrinths.

The genius of traditional labyrinth patterns is that you cannot tell exactly where you are on the path as you walk. At times it seems like you are getting close to the center, but then you pass it by. At other times it feels like you are approaching the end, but it is an illusion. Ideally, at some point you surrender to the process, immerse yourself in the walking, and simply follow the path. You are present with your own movement and you watch as the path shifts and turns. This is a powerful metaphor for life: we do the thing in front of us, and it is impossible to say with accuracy where we are in the journey.

Like mindfulness practice, a labyrinth walk can appear simplistic. After all, you are just walking on a predetermined path. However, the experience can be quite profound. The movement combined with not knowing exactly where you are on the path at any given moment allows you to let go and be present for the experience. Although I have participated in indoor labyrinth walks, outdoor labyrinths are preferable. They provide the additional gift of experiencing a connection to the green world.

Traditional labyrinths can be set up as a permanent walk made of rocks, bricks, or some other material, but they can also be set up with ropes or chalk. Powdered chalk used for sporting events can be purchased at a sporting goods store relatively inexpensively.

You can set up any walking path with ropes and/or chalk. Don't be limited by the pattern of the traditional labyrinth. Any designated path will allow you to let go of thinking where your feet have to be next or making decisions about which way to turn. That creates space to simply be in the rhythm of walking; you can be mindful of what is unfolding in front of you. However, depending on the pattern, it may be obvious where the beginning and end of the path are—this detracts from one of the benefits of the labyrinth.

~~~~~~~

The power of the labyrinth is that you are walking in an outdoor space and yet, the path is laid out for you so there are no decisions to be made. It is just one foot in front of the other. Practice any of these suggested techniques:

- Keep your eyes open and gently scan the area to take in trees, the rest of the natural world, and also other walkers. See them all as part of the oneness.

- Keep your eyes lowered and follow the path, watching as each foot rises up and then comes back down to connect with the earth.

- Focus on breathing as you walk. Synchronize your breath with your steps.

- Walk with a phrase that helps you tune in to the beauty around you, as in the last exploration. For example, "I am grateful for this labyrinth and the green world."

- Walk with a question. For example, "What am I hearing in this moment? What am I seeing in this moment?" Then tune in to your sight or hearing.

Labyrinths as a Group Activity or Public Event

When I lived in Pennsylvania, my friends and I created a series of large, luminaria-lit labyrinths over a couple of years. Some were on private property and some were at a public park. Walking outdoors under the moonlight enhanced the meditation. Here are some things to consider if you are working on a public outdoor labyrinth:

- The most inexpensive way to lay out the labyrinth is with chalk or rope.

- Directions and designs for patterns can be found online.

- Making the paths at least two feet wide makes it easier for people to walk through them.

- Traditional luminarias are candles inside paper bags weighted down with sand. This may or may not be a good idea depending on where you live. In Pennsylvania, where it was often wet, this was not a problem. In dryer parts of the country, you may want to consider an alternative like electric or solar tea lights.

- You'll want to provide information about the walking process if you are hosting a public event. Don't assume people know how to navigate a labyrinth. Ask people to walk silently and attune themselves to both the labyrinth and the space they are walking in. It is easier to sense the energy of a place when there is silence.

- If possible, set up an area away from the labyrinth for people to gather and talk. People who are waiting to walk or have finished walking may want to talk about what they experienced. It is helpful to have it out of range of those still walking the path. When my friends and I created our labyrinths, we set up a hot chocolate and tea station away from the labyrinth and people were naturally drawn there.

- Quiet meditative music or simple drumming rhythms can enhance walkers' ability to stay focused, as well as masking any traffic or other distractions in the distance.

- Limit picture taking. This electronic intrusion takes away from the mindfulness of the event and the walk. To accommodate the people who want to take photos, I recommend setting aside specific times that is allowed, possibly at the beginning or end of the event. Make sure to post that information on flyers and on a large sign as people approach the event and explain the reason why. It is not an arbitrary rule, but instead a way to help everyone be more attuned to the moment.

Exploration
QIGONG IN THE GARDEN

Type of Exploration: Movement

Supplies Needed:
- Comfortable clothing

Ideal Setting: A garden or park where you feel comfortable

Child Friendly: Yes

When I was first introduced to qigong, it was like a key fitting into a lock. I had already discovered movement meditation through dancing and drumming, but qigong carried with it a structured approach and hundreds (or thousands, depending on who tells the story) of years of history to back it up. There were prescribed movements and sequences to experiment with.

Qigong is part of traditional Chinese healing practices, and as such there is an understanding that the world is made of energy. It is recognized as a mind-body practice that releases stress and helps people tune in to presence.

Chinese healing arts did not develop in a vacuum. They were immersed in the natural world and the seasons. There is an understanding that different qualities of energy are at work depending on the time of year, and we can tune in to them with focused attention.

Some qigong movements are very complicated, but the three presented here are easily learned and ideal for garden settings. The ease of learning the movement allows you to focus on the energetic qualities of the garden as you engage with the practice.

All of these movements are done standing. However, they can be modified by sitting in a chair if needed. The movement can be done with eyes open or closed. Keep in mind that it will be experienced differently depending on which way you do it. It may be easier to do these movements with your eyes closed to start so that you can focus on learning the exercise. All exercises have the same beginning position.

Beginning Position
- Stand with your feet shoulder width apart. Distribute your weight evenly between your feet.
- Feel or imagine your connection to the earth.
- Imagine a string connected to the top of your head. It is pulling you gently upward so that you are standing tall, but don't become rigid. Your shoulders and arms are limp and relaxed.
- Tilt your pelvis forward to create an invisible line from the top of your head to your pelvis.
- Keep your knees slightly bent and relaxed.
- From the top of your head, imagine waves of relaxation flowing down through your body. With each wave, feel your muscles relaxing more. Feel the tightness flow out of your face and neck. You may want to roll your neck a little as the imaginary wave comes through. Feel your shoulders sinking with each wave. (We hold a lot of tension in our shoulders, so pay a lot of attention to letting them become loose.)

Let the waves flow through your body. You should be relaxed, with just enough muscle tension to keep you upright.

Gathering Energy

Begin by taking a deep breath. Be aware of the air coming in through your nose and filling your lungs. Slowly breathe out and, with each exhale, know that your body is releasing toxins and parts of the air that you do not need. Take three or four deep breaths to start.

As you begin your next breath, turn your palms to face outward (keeping them at your sides) and slowly bring them out from your sides in an arc, almost as if you are drawing part of a circle. Your palms continue to rise until your fingertips meet over your head. As you do this movement, imagine that you are scooping up all of the green space's positive energy. At the end of your inhale, hold your breath for just a moment. Then, slowly and on the exhale, bring your hands down along the front of your body. Your fingertips and palms should be facing the ground. As you do this movement, feel the energy from the garden flow through your body. Return your hands to your sides.

Repeat this cycle of movement at least three times.

Once you feel you have somewhat mastered this exercise with closed eyes, try doing it with your eyes open. As in some of the walking meditations, imagine that you are part of the wholeness of this scene. You are not an isolated human experiencing a garden. Instead, you are simply one other organism in a multitude of organisms, all exchanging energy. See if you can touch that awareness.

Touching Heaven and Earth

Begin with the beginning position. On an inhale, slowly bring both hands up and in front of your abdomen as if holding a soccer ball. Breathe in and out a few times. As you do, imagine or feel the energy between your hands. Then, on an inhale, turn your right hand out and away from you until your palm is facing up. Push your hand up gently toward the sky, reaching it above your head. At the same time, keep your left palm facing down at your side. Push your left palm gently toward the earth. Feel this stretch. Make sure you are not locking your elbows. Hold this position for a moment. As you do, feel or imagine the connection of energy between the earth and the rest of the universe. While holding this position, know that energy is traveling through your palms in both directions.

Each day electromagnetic and solar energy wash over us and the planet. Gravity from the earth travels up from the planet into the atmosphere. We are touching both heaven and earth. Feel the connection that exists.

On an exhale, release and allow your hands to float back down to the position of holding a ball in front of you. Repeat this movement, but switch the position of your hands by raising your left palm toward the sky.

Repeat this exercise on both sides three times.

This is a powerful exercise that can promote awareness of your connection to a much wider universe.

Channeling Earth Energy

In this exercise, you can feel the energy of the earth coming up through your feet and body and then out to the planet. You will become a channel for healing and positive energy.

Stand in the beginning position, then slowly bring your hands in front of your body so that your palms are facing upward and your fingertips are touching. Your arms are not raised, but relaxed in front of you. Your elbows should be slightly bent.

On an inhale, slowly bring your hands up the front of your body. As you do that, feel or imagine the energy from the planet coming up through the center of your feet, through your legs, knees, and pelvis. As your hands begin to move, they are pulling the energy up like a magnet from the earth. The energy catches up to your hands. This healing energy continues up through your stomach, chest, throat, and head.

When your hands reach the top of your head, turn your palms up and out. The healing energy flows out through your hands and into the garden and surrounding area as you exhale. You can imagine this as a fountain or shower of energy. Feel it and see it.

Take another full breath while maintaining this position. Feel the energy come up through your body to your hands. This time on the exhale, bring your hands down to your sides in an arc. As you do, see and feel the energy being distributed all around you.

Repeat this movement cycle three times.

Reflecting on Movement

Our bodies are the vehicle through which we engage with the world. It seems obvious that awareness of our body's movements should be included in mindfulness practice. However, when I think back to my early days of meditation, it was more as a disembodied brain than as a complete entity. I couldn't see it at the time, but I often ignored signals of both distress and joy. Mindfulness practices can shine a light on how we exist in our bodies and how we are interconnected with the green world and each other.

three
CREATIVE EXPLORATIONS

Human beings are creative creatures. It is deeply satisfying to watch something new emerge from our hands and energy. I love creating things from my garden. Creativity takes many forms. It might be the everyday creations of preparing a meal from garden produce, or it might be drying herbs for tea or to give as gifts. Herbal pillows, oils, salves, soaps, handmade paper, and note cards have all materialized from my garden.

This chapter includes explorations that we traditionally think of as crafting, but that also include harvesting and routine garden tasks. That's because gardening itself is a creative activity. We make decisions about colors and combinations, pour our energy into a garden plot, and lovingly tend plants. There is a sense of accomplishment when they thrive. Creation of any kind can be done in a mindful way.

The difference between simply crafting and crafting with a mindful focus is the intention and attention. There are an infinite number of creative activities that you can engage in. However, especially at the beginning, you should aim for simplicity. If you are just learning a new craft and it is complicated, that may not be the best activity to practice mindful focus. The craft and culinary activities in this section are easy entry points to mindfulness.

When I've introduced these activities in mindfulness workshops, participants are often surprised by the discoveries they make. We are used to over-laying our daily activities with other activities and distractions. We listen to music or podcasts as we prepare dinner. We talk on the phone as we are pulling weeds. Sometimes it feels like our culture demands this doubling up of activities. When you take the time to simply focus on one task, you might have a revelation as you notice how much you don't pay attention to.

The activities I've selected here are based on a few criteria:

- They are easy to do. This is important because if there is a steep learning curve, it will be hard to practice mindfulness. If you choose your own creative garden projects to do in a mindful way, choose something simple to start. The idea is to have the garden be a doorway to mindfulness. You want the door to swing open easily; you should not be struggling to push on it.

- Each of the crafts easily makes something beautiful, interesting, and/or flavorful. If you pick a craft that is difficult, your self-judgment is likely to creep in, telling you your work is not good enough. That leads to a whole cascade of feelings that will pull you away from mindfulness.

- The supplies needed are reasonably priced and easy to find.

- Most of these explorations are easy enough to include children.

Reminders and Suggestions

- Don't assume that because these explorations are easy, they are not a deep way to practice. It's the simplicity that makes an easy entry point for paying attention. Be open to learning from these experiences. If your last experience with any of these activities was as a child, don't shy away from them. Embrace the idea of a simple activity being extraordinary.

- Any activity can be done in a mindful way.

- Silence is a key part of doing these practices. It allows you to tune in to the activity in a more focused way. Take off the headset, turn off the phone, and be present for the activity. If you are doing an activity with children, explain why the activity is done in silence. Depending on the age of the children, you may want to keep the activity short so they can have success with silence. Alternatively, if you think your children will be challenged by completing a whole activity in silence, designate only part of the activity to mindfulness. Set a timer to engage with the project in a mindful way, and once the timer goes off, you can talk about the experience and complete the project.

- The preparation activities can be part of the mindfulness practice, or not. At the beginning, it might be best to limit your practice to the actual craft and then as you gain proficiency, include the preparation activities as well.

Exploration
LEAF RUBBINGS

Type of Exploration: Creative craft

Supplies Needed:
- Paper of various weights
- Crayons, colored pencils, and/or chalk
- A hard surface
- Tape
- Journal or paper
- Pen or pencil

Ideal Setting: A garden or other green space where you can collect leaves

Child Friendly: Yes

Leaf rubbings are a beautiful mindfulness craft project. As a bonus, the finished product can be used as note cards, gift tags, or invitations. They are created by placing leaves under paper and rubbing pencils or crayons over the paper to make an image of the leaves. There are endless variations.

Give some thought to the supplies needed and, if possible, try out a few different kinds. Having at least a few different weights of paper before you start is a good idea. Different weights of paper create different results. Copy paper may work with thin leaves but will tear with thicker ones. Paper for sketching is often a good choice, as it has some substance to it without being overly thick. Sketch paper can be found at a craft store or online. Watercolor paper will be too thick for this activity.

Colored pencils and crayons work well as the rubbing tools. Thick crayons are easier to handle, especially for younger children, but regular-size crayons will work as well. Chalk can also be used, but the finished rubbing won't be permanent.

You'll need a hard surface and tape to fasten the paper down. Assemble all your materials and decide on your hard surface before you begin the activity.

～～～～～

Tune in to the garden space. Breathe and center yourself. Walk slowly through or around the green space, paying attention to the texture and shape of the leaves. Begin to gather interesting leaves or leaves that call out to you in some way.

When you have enough to choose from, return to the area where you'll be sitting. Intentionally arrange leaves on your hard surface. Experiment with placing leaves right-side up and upside down. Veins in leaves are often more prominent on the reverse side.

When you've finished arranging your leaves, tape your paper over the leaves so it doesn't move as you are creating the rubbing. Gently begin to shade over the paper. Pressing harder or lighter will produce different results. Be present with the entire experience: the feel of the crayon or pencil in your hand, the texture of the paper, and the sound of your crayon or pencil creating the rubbing. Watch the magic of the leaf's shape coming to life on the paper.

Record your thoughts in your journal. What did you discover while collecting the leaves? What did you discover when you watched the leaves appear on the paper as your hands moved? What felt different about the leaves when you saw them as rubbings? How successful were you in remaining attentive to the process?

For future explorations, try different colored paper and/or different colored pencils. White pencils on black paper make a striking combination. You could also use many different colors of pencils or crayons on the same rubbing.

Exploration
SOLAR PRINTS

Type of Exploration: Creative craft

Supplies Needed:
- Solar print paper
- Small tub filled with water
- Towel
- Journal or paper
- Pen or pencil

Ideal Setting: A green space or garden where you have permission to pick plants

Child Friendly: Yes

Solar prints are made with paper that has been treated to react with the sun, creating an image where the paper is shaded. This paper is easily available online and at many toy and craft stores. It creates sun prints of cobalt blue and white.

Before you begin, gather your supplies and decide on your work area. You may want to create your designs in the shade and then move them into the sun. The solar print paper comes in a dark envelope. The paper will react with sunlight as soon as it is out of the wrapper, so don't take it out until you are ready to place your design. Be prepared for the wind. Most kits come with a clear acrylic sheet to place over your design so the wind won't take it away. However, I've purchased some kits that don't include it, and if you are using thick leaves and plants, the acrylic won't help anyway. You can set up boxes around your design as windbreakers, or place the design inside an open box as long as the sun can still reach it. You'll also need water nearby, as the paper needs to be immersed in water to set the print.

~~~~~~~

As with the leaf rubbings, center yourself before beginning. Then walk through and around the garden, noticing plants that would make interesting shadow art. Collect a variety of leaves, flowers, and garden materials so you have some choices when you begin to design. Pay attention to their look and fragrance.

Return to your work area and arrange the plants on a flat surface in an interesting way, taking into consideration the size of the paper. When you are ready, remove one of the solar print pages from the black envelope and transfer your design onto it. You'll need to work quickly but attentively. If you are using the acrylic sheet, place it over the design and set the design in the sun.

Once placed in the sun, the blue paper begins to turn white. The leaves and plant material on the paper will block the sun and that part of the paper will remain blue. This is the perfect mindfulness activity because there is a waiting period as the design is created. Sit and observe as the paper's reaction with the sun takes place. In sunny weather, it is a short wait time, but if you are doing this exploration when it is cloudy, the wait time could be fifteen minutes. You might intentionally choose a cloudier day to ensure a longer observation period.

Once the exposed paper has turned white, it is time to set the print by immersing it in water. Gently remove all plant materials and dip the paper in the tub of water, swishing it around for at least forty-five seconds. (If you prefer, you can hold the paper under running water from a sink or hose.) Observe the paper as this process is happening. The colors reverse. What was white becomes blue and what was blue becomes white.

Once the color reversal has taken place, lay the wet paper on a towel to dry. Take time to observe the final design.

Record observations in your journal. What did you experience with each phase? How did the final product compare to your expectations? How successful were you in remaining attentive to the process?

Exploration
BOTANICALS AS STAMPS AND BRUSHES

Type of Exploration: Creative craft

Supplies Needed:
- Scissors
- Paper
- Paints or ink

- Knife (optional)
- Cutting board (optional)
- Journal or paper
- Pen or pencil

Ideal Setting: Your own garden or a place you have permission to gather plants

Child Friendly: Yes

Another way to engage with plants in a creative way is to use them as tools to apply paint or ink to paper. The feathery leaves of yarrow, fennel, parsley, and cosmos make beautiful designs on paper. More rigid parts of plants can be used as stamps by dipping them in paint or ink and stamping the image on paper. Seed heads of coneflowers and sunflowers are a good starting point for stamps that do not require a lot of preparation. Vegetables and fruits cut in half also make unique stamping tools; try peppers, okra, eggplant, zucchini, apple, or pear.

Set up your work area before you begin. You'll need to decide if you will use paint or ink. (I've had success using both.) You can make your own ink/paint pads with a shallow container, a sponge, and paints or inks of your choice. Craft stores sell ready-to-use ink pads for stamping. Different weights and types of paper will create different results.

~~~~~~~~~~

Begin by tuning in to the garden. As with other activities, take your time. Bring your awareness to each plant in front of you as you decide what you'll use and thank each plant as you collect it. Once you have your plant material selected, head back to your work area. If you are creating stamps, you may need to cut vegetables or fruits to expose the inside pattern. Slicing horizontally or vertically will give you different patterns. Stay observant as you work.

It can be a discovery process to figure out which plants work well for printing/stamping. In the fall you will have more materials to work with, but you can find interesting stamping material almost any time of the year.

Print or stamp your material onto paper. Experiment with different types of paper to see what you like best. When you've finished, allow your art to dry. The finished products can be beautiful wrapping paper, note cards, or other gifts.

Record your thoughts in your journal. What did you discover during this creative process? What did you learn about the plants you were using to make art? How successful were you in staying mindful?

Exploration
JUDGMENT-FREE DRAWING

Type of Exploration: Creative craft

Supplies Needed:
- Paper for drawing or a small sketchbook
- Colored pencils

Ideal Setting: Any green space

Child Friendly: Maybe, depending on the child

Drawing is a great way to cultivate full awareness of the green world. In chapter 1, drawing was used as a tool to get to know a plant. With that activity there was not a final product. This activity differs in that you'll have a completed drawing of a plant. The potential problem is that some of us are harsh critics when it comes to our own drawing skills. For that reason, I was hesitant about including this mindfulness activity. If you can set aside self-judgment, then proceed.

Although you can draw on any type of paper, it adds to the experience to use quality paper made for sketching, available at any craft store. Paper comes in all sizes. I recommend starting small, especially if you do not consider yourself an artist, because it is less intimidating.

~~~~~~~

Ground yourself, breathe, and take time to identify a plant you'd like to draw. Find a place to sit that is comfortable for drawing. You might choose a plant simply because you can sit comfortably while you sketch it.

Begin by observing the plant and considering what parts you would like to capture. You may want to do a detailed sketch of the entire plant, or you might want to focus on a flower or branch. Perhaps you want to focus on the overall structure of the plant and not capture the tiny details. Be intentional about your choices. What are you seeing and what are you choosing to highlight on the paper?

As you begin, remember to breathe. Frame this activity as a way to communicate with the plant, not as a task to complete.

Joann Flick, a program director for the Montana State Library, hikes frequently in Glacier National Park. She shared a similar practice with me that involves painting rather than drawing. She keeps paints and small sheets of watercolor paper in her backpack. As she is hiking, she stops to make tiny paintings of plants and wildlife and often shares them with friends or uses them as postcards.

Whether you are painting or drawing, the activity helps sharpen your vision and awareness of the green world. It helps you tune in to the smallest details of beauty.

In your journal, record what you discovered about the plant as you were drawing.

Exploration
GARDEN MANDALAS

Type of Exploration: Creative craft

Supplies Needed:
- Plants, twigs, and stones from your garden or another green space
- String or chalk to outline the circle (optional)
- Poster board, cardboard, or plain cloth to be used as a canvas (optional)

Ideal Setting: A quiet green space where you have permission to pick plants

Child Friendly: Yes

Mandalas are circular designs that originated in Buddhist practices. Traditional mandalas include Buddhist symbols and prayers. In common usage, a mandala is any circular design that assists with mindfulness. As a meditation tool, the mandala has a focal point that draws our eyes repeatedly back to the center, assisting with staying focused. Both the creation of the mandala and meditating on the mandala are mindful activities.

The circle is a sacred symbol in many spiritual traditions. It may be a natural human impulse to appreciate and create circular designs. A few years ago, while at the park with my granddaughter and her friend, the girls spontaneously began creating a nature mandala. They were playing with some pinecones and arranged them in a pattern on the ground. Suddenly they were creating a free-form mandala with the pinecones and other plant materials in the park. Once they got started, they ran through the park looking for other items that would fit with their design. There was a natural progression. They added material until they felt they had the symmetry right and then stopped to admire what they had created.

On a recent walk I discovered another spontaneous mandala. It looked as though it was the work of another child artist. The circular and symmetrical design combined plants with found items like an orange peel and a gum wrapper. The young artist placed it where others could appreciate it: in the middle of the sidewalk.

We can experience the power of mandalas through posters, books, coloring pages, and our own drawings, but creating our own garden mandalas engages all our senses. It helps us tune in to the natural world and each plant that we are using as part of the design. It is an opportunity to be aware of the different aspects of a plant and how the plant fits into the larger whole. Working with a plant-based mandala also mirrors one of the outcomes of Buddhist sand mandalas; after they are completed, they are swept away, reminding us of the impermanence of all things. Our green mandalas will deteriorate and can then be composted.

~~~~~~~

Begin by deciding the location and size of your mandala. The size will determine the amount of time you'll need. Creating a mandala does not have to be a long process, but you do want to allow enough time to appreciate the plants and the experience. Creating a large mandala will require more time and plants (or larger pieces of each plant). For a solitary mandala, a circle one to three feet in diameter is a good start.

If you are creating the mandala directly on the ground, string or chalk can be used to define the outer boundaries. A piece of solid-colored fabric or cardboard can also be laid on the ground as a canvas to help define the space and make the design stand out. If kneeling or sitting on the ground is difficult, a mandala can also be created on a table, either indoors or out.

You can approach this activity in one of two ways:

1. Collecting all your plant and natural materials first, then creating the mandala
2. Collecting materials and creating the design simultaneously

I prefer the first method: gathering all my materials before I begin creating the design. It allows me to create a palette of colors, textures, and fragrances. Then I move to creating something on my canvas.

Practicing intentionality and awareness as you collect your plants and create your design is what makes this a mindful activity. When collecting plants, give thanks to each plant as you snip off parts to be included in the design. Be attentive to other objects in the garden that could be included in the design: stones with unique shapes and colors, twigs, dried stalks, tree leaves, etc.

As you create the design, each choice of plant and placement is a conscious decision. You are not throwing a design together, but instead honoring a green space and allowing the plant energies to help you decide on placement.

Be attentive to the texture and fragrance of the plants. Notice how the design shifts and changes with each addition. Keep your attention on the flow of moments.

There will be a point when the mandala feels done; you've placed the last plant and there is a feeling of completion. Sit with the mandala and tune in to the energy of your co-creation. You may want to meditate near your mandala or record the process in your journal.

Depending on where you've created the mandala, materials can be left for the wind and rain to disperse, or you can add materials to a compost.

Creating a Group Mandala

I often include the creation of nature mandalas in mindfulness workshops as a silent group activity. Participants love handling the natural materials and watching the design come to life. The added aspect of creating with a team allows us to practice mindfulness while interacting with others, a great skill for all of life. Group mandala creation can be incorporated into rituals, celebrations, and memorials as a way to deepen group connection.

Tips for creating a group mandala include:

- Think about the number of people involved and map out a large enough space.

- When done as a group activity, it's easier to have the plants and materials chosen ahead of time. You can invite people to bring materials with them, but be prepared with enough for everyone.

- If you live in a hot and dry area, plants should be kept cool and moist so they maintain their structure after they are picked and before the mandala creation.

- Include plants with different textures and fragrances.

- In winter, use the stems of plants that hang on to their unique fragrances like sage, lavender, and lemon balm. Include natural items from the supermarket like carrots, carrot tops, celery, and various colors of dried beans.

- Steer clear of plants that are common allergens.

- Some of the easiest plants to collect in abundance are considered weeds. They are plentiful and many have interesting leaves, flowers, and shapes. Do use common sense when collecting weeds. Some cause skin irritation or allergic reactions. If you are not familiar with the plant, look it up or don't include it.

- Rocks, sticks, pinecones, and other natural products can be used in addition to garden materials.

- Choose some meditative instrumental music to play as a soundscape for the activity.

- When you are ready to create the design, items should be spread out and visible as a palette for artists to choose from.
- Provide everyone with information about the mandala creation before beginning. If you are sending invitations, provide information about the mandala creation and why you are choosing this activity. Don't assume people will know what you are trying to accomplish or how to participate. Include information like:
  - This is a mindful practice.
  - This is a silent activity—participating without talking will allow everyone to be more present with the plants and the experience.
  - Cell phones should be turned off.
  - When the mandala is completed, everyone should take some time to just *be* with their creation. View it from different angles and notice all the intricacies. Often at workshops, people want to photograph what they have created. That is fine, but I encourage people to simply be with the mandala before bringing out your phones.

Whether you are creating a solitary or group mandala, something new emerges in these moments. Take some time to be conscious of that.

Exploration
MAKING HERBAL TEA WITH FRESH HERBS

Type of Exploration: Culinary creation

Supplies Needed:
- Scissors
- Teapot or one-quart glass canning jar
- Strainer
- Teacups
- Journal or paper
- Pen or pencil
- Agave, sweetener, or other tea additives (optional)

Ideal Setting: A garden space where you can collect herbs

Child Friendly: Yes

When I was a child, I remember my friends and I making potions by picking lots of wildflowers, adding them to water in a pail, and stirring. This might be a developmental stage that children go through, as my children and grandchildren invented similar games. Plants seem to call us to pick, mix, and stir. When you think about it, what is herbal tea–making but a kind of potion brewing?

The word *tea* originally referred to a hot water infusion of the plant *Camellia sinensis*. However, it is now used for herbal infusions as well. Some herbalists make a distinction between teas and infusions, with teas being brewed for a shorter time and considered more pleasant to drink. Infusions are brewed longer, have a stronger taste, and are usually intended as an herbal remedy.

Any of the following garden herbs make great teas: lemon balm, spearmint, chocolate mint, chamomile, anise, fennel, bee balm, raspberry leaves, and sage. They can also be combined to make your own unique blends. Tasting and comparing flavors can be its own mindful exploration.

~~~~~~~~

Assemble your teapot, strainer, and cups before you head out to your green space. (A one-quart glass canning jar, available in most supermarkets, makes a good teapot if you don't have one.) Once you are outside, take a moment to ground yourself. You may already know which plant(s) you are using for tea, but if not, walk through the garden and observe the available plants as you decide. Then thank the plant(s) and begin harvesting. Pay attention to the touch and fragrance of the plant(s) as you do. Stay focused with an intentional statement such as: "I am tuning in to each plant I choose for tea making."

For each pot of tea (using four cups, or a quart, of water), you will need about ¾ cup of fresh leaves. This is not an exact science, so experiment to see what works best. Herbs can be rinsed in a colander if they have dirt or dust on them, then pat them dry. At each step, take your time and stay focused on the task at hand.

As you measure out the appropriate amount of water for your tea, be mindful of how this clean water came to you. Do you live in a city that pipes water to your home, or do you have a well that provides you with water? Where did the water come from originally? Be aware of the cycle of water on the planet that supports all life. Be thankful for the water as well as the plants. Also consider how you are heating the water. Be aware of the gift of whatever energy source is allowing you to heat the water to make tea.

Begin boiling the water. As you are waiting for the water to boil, pick up the leaves and tear them into small parts to release their flavors and extracts. Be present with this process as you pull apart the leaves. You can use a focusing phrase like: "I am preparing leaves and flowers to release their flavors into this tea."

When the water is boiling, add the leaves. Let brew for ten minutes. One advantage to using a glass canning jar or any glass teapot is that you can watch the water slowly change into tea. Pay attention to this transformation. I love this part. The plant is giving up its flavors and essential ingredients to the water, making tea for you. If you don't have a glass teapot, this can still be a period of mindful awareness. Focus on your breath and the fragrance. Know that tea is being made.

Once the tea has brewed, pour it into cups, paying attention to the color and fragrance and the flow of liquid. Let the tea cool for a few moments, continuing your mindful attention. As you bring the cup to your lips, allow yourself to take in the fragrances again. Take a deep breath and sip your tea. Let the feel of the cup touching your lips, the fragrance, and the first taste wash over you. Continue drinking.

Record any thoughts you have in your journal. How was this experience different from your usual tea making and drinking? What did you discover?

Exploration
HARVESTING AND PREPARING FOOD

Type of Exploration: Culinary creation

Supplies Needed:
- Scissors or knife
- Colander for washing plants
- Journal or paper
- Pen or pencil

Ideal Setting: A garden where you have permission to harvest plants

Child Friendly: Yes

Sometimes people will tell me they don't have time to practice mindfulness. While it is true that a sitting meditation practice provides good experience to take forward into our lives, it's also true that we have innumerable ways to practice mindfulness with our everyday tasks.

Harvesting, washing produce, and chopping vegetables all are great activities to practice presence and gratitude for the bounty. They are simple, easily accessible activities and they have a deep connection to the garden. However, don't assume you will be mindful just because you are in the garden. Set an intention about the number of minutes you will stay focused. If you are new to mindfulness, start small. It is better to build on small successes than to tell yourself you'll do an hour and get distracted.

Probably the biggest challenge with these activities is that we have done them hundreds of times before and it is easy to slide into inattention. Take the time to ground and center yourself before you begin, and use focus statements to stay alert to the process: "I am thoughtfully preparing food from my garden. I am grateful for the garden harvest and the time to prepare it."

After you have harvested and prepared food, record any thoughts you have in your journal. How was this practice different from your usual practice of harvesting or preparing food? What did you discover?

A Word About Big Harvests

I will confess that the times I am challenged with staying mindful are when too much of everything needs to be harvested immediately. The big producers in my yard are currants, raspberries, tomatoes, and squash of every kind. I am always thankful for the amount of food I get from a few plants. However, I can sometimes slide into feeling frazzled about harvesting them all. I don't want any to go to waste.

What helps me in those situations is first reminding myself that I am not a farmer and my livelihood does not depend on the harvest. I can consciously let go and bless the birds and wildlife with some of the produce, which they will happily accept. I can also invite friends over to share the harvest.

Another tool I use is consciously refocusing on what is happening in the garden rather than the task of harvesting. I turn my attention to the magic that has just taken place in my yard. Here in this space, I took a tiny seed or plant, placed it in the ground, nurtured it, and together with sunshine, water, and care, the plant is providing me with real food, full of vital energy and nutrients. I am grateful for this backyard miracle.

If I still feel frazzled, I work with a reminder phrase like: "I am thankful for this plant that is providing so much bounty for my family and friends."

Exploration
ENGAGING ROUTINE GARDENING TASKS IN A MINDFUL WAY

Type of Exploration: Creative craft and sensory

Supplies Needed:
- Gardening tools, depending on the activity
- Journal or paper
- Pen or pencil
- Timer (optional)

Ideal Setting: A garden

Child Friendly: Maybe, depending on the child

Soil preparation, sowing seeds, mulching, watering, and weeding—the routine tasks of tending a garden can all be embraced in a mindful way. I placed this exploration in this chapter because tending the garden itself is a creative endeavor. Like the previous entry about harvesting and preparing food, the goal is to be present with our usual garden chores.

Engaging routine tasks in a mindful way is one of the easiest entry points for mindful practice because they are something we do often. They are also challenging because we think of them as rather mundane. The familiarity of the task makes us discount them. Because we've done these things hundreds of times, it is also easy to slide out of mindfulness. We put our body on autopilot and our attention drifts to the grocery list or the phone call we need to make.

Another challenge is that routine tasks are part of our to-do list. They are things we need to get done. Most of us feel some pressure to accomplish the tasks on the list and move on. If there is a lot to do, it can be harder to focus.

So how do we turn a regular task into a mindfulness activity? With intention and commitment. To begin, define what task you'll be doing, then decide on a specific time period that you will stay mindful to the work at hand. Remember to let go of your electronic connections. It's common practice to listen to music or a podcast while doing routine tasks, but turn those off for the mindfulness part of your task. If you are weeding, take five minutes to just pull weeds. Experience what it feels like to focus on the garden and the task at hand.

Success contributes to more success, so start small. Starting small allows us to stretch our mindfulness muscles and then let them relax. If we do this continuously, we become stronger with our attention, just as we do with our real muscles.

~~~~~~~~

Begin with deep, connecting breaths. When you start gardening, be attentive to the whole experience: the touch of the seeds, soil, or rake; the experience of using your body to move the earth or leaves; the air on your face and the sun on your body. See how long you can ride the flow of present moments—even if it's just for a short time—before being thrown off course.

Whenever your attention is pulled away, gently refocus yourself with a statement like: "I am pulling weeds" or "I am planting seeds."

Please try this one! Head out to the garden and fully immerse yourself in one gardening task for five minutes. Record the experience in your journal. How was this different from your usual garden tasks? What did you experience? What did you discover?

Reflecting on Creativity

There are countless ways to engage mindfully and creatively with the garden. As you explore the ideas in this chapter, you may be drawn to some activities more than others; start with those and see where they take you. You may also have insights on how to change an activity to deepen your practice and awareness. Listen to your internal suggestions. Remember as you dive into these activities that creativity is not the sole domain of professional artists. Humans are an inventive and imaginative species. When we are open to inspiration with a mindful focus, we can step back, let go of judgment about the final product, and experience the flow of creating.

four

ELEMENTAL EXPLORATIONS

Earth, air, fire, and water—the ancient Greeks divided the world into these primal elements. I remember learning this fact in elementary school, but sadly it was presented in a dismissive way. The ancient Greeks did not have the tools to break the world into molecules, atoms, and subatomic particles. Their categories were born of observation and rich interactions with the natural world. If we adjust our view, we might see that there is wisdom and poetry in their divisions and a recognition that the earth itself is sacred. When we take a moment to consider it, how could it be otherwise? Life is made possible by these four elements, even if they can be subdivided into tinier parts; nourishment springs from the earth, breath is dependent on air, life emerged from water, and the fiery sun is just the right distance from our planet to make life possible.

In addition to earth, air, fire, and water, there is a fifth element—spirit. Spirit is the consciousness embodied in humans and other sentient beings. Through spirit we can embrace a mindfulness practice that attunes us to the natural world. Tapping into that awareness, we begin to see the interconnectedness of all things—how the elements are connected, to another and to each of us.

There are, of course other ways to map the energetic world. (As an example, traditional Chinese medicine has five energetic elements: wood, fire, earth, metal, and water.) This is just one path, but the four elements of earth, air, fire, and water make intuitive sense to me. Working in my garden with my hands in the soil, I am connected to earth. I am outside in the element of air. The sun provides the energy for my plants to create their own food through photosynthesis, and the water enables them to move nutrients through their green bodies.

One of my most vivid memories of the elements in full force was a winter solstice celebration my circle held (or tried to hold) at sunrise on Lake Erie. We met at a lakeside parking lot before dawn with the frigid wind howling, sleet and sand stinging our faces. We attempted to stay with our planned ritual but lasted only about ten minutes. The wind tried to knock us off our feet, our chants dissolving in the roar. We stayed long enough to welcome the sun as it crested the horizon and then ran for the shelter of our cars, followed by coffee and pancakes at a warm and cozy restaurant. As short as our celebration was, the visceral memory of that morning so many years ago stays with me. The raw power of each of the elements was vividly on display. It was invigorating to be in the center of that power and humbling to realize our small place in the plan. The elements are often not that dramatic, but they are there for each of us to experience if we just tune in.

The activities that follow are a way to align ourselves with each of the elements in the green world. The idea is to cultivate a mindful awareness of their presence—real and allegorical—and explore their energy, vibration, symbolism, and effect on our lives.

Exploration
SENSING EARTH

Type of Exploration: Elemental

Supplies Needed:
- Journal or paper
- Pen or pencil

Ideal Setting: A garden or other green space

Child Friendly: Yes

This activity is an exploration of earth's healing energy. The earth supports us in many ways. It makes life possible. It is obvious that plants and trees are rooted in the earth, but in a way humans are also rooted to the earth through gravity.

We explored some of these concepts by walking and sensing gravity in chapter 2. In this activity, we are simply still and attentive as we tune in to that energy.

~~~~~~~~~~

Find a way to be close to the earth in a garden or green space. Sit or lie on the ground. If it's not possible to sit on the ground, use a chair. Be still and take some time to just be present in this green space. If possible, place your hands on the ground. It can be helpful to state your intention: "I am consciously attuning to earth energy. I am open to sensing and learning from this energy."

Bring your attention to whatever parts of your body are in contact with the earth and sense that connection. If your hands are touching the earth, focus your attention on the center of your palms. There is a palpable energy that emanates from the earth. If you don't feel the energy at first, stay with it. Be patient and don't give up too soon. It may be subtle at first. Modern life is so loud and noisy that it takes some adjusting to quiet down and sense subtle energy.

It helps to remember that this is not an imaginary energy. The earth has a gravitational and electromagnetic field. Know that they are there even if you cannot yet tune in. If your mind wanders, bring yourself back to awareness by repeating your intention.

In your journal, record any insights and discoveries about earth energy.

Exploration
TUNING IN TO SOIL

Type of Exploration: Elemental

Supplies Needed:
- Journal or paper
- Pen or pencil
- Garden trowel

Ideal Setting: A garden or other green space where you have permission to work with a small amount of soil

Child Friendly: Yes

This activity is a meditation and observation on soil. Soil is not just a holding material for plants; it is a living system of organisms and minerals that nourish and make the growth of plants possible. A part of soil is made of the rocks and minerals in the upper layer of the earth's crust. It also consists of water, air, living and decaying plant materials, and tiny organisms including ants, worms, fungi, and bacteria. Even as gardeners, we sometimes are so busy tending to plants that we don't fully tune in to this living system. If you have your own garden (or are using a friend's), you can explore soil in a more mindful way.

~~~~~~~~~

Sit comfortably on the ground or in a chair. With your trowel, turn over a small portion of soil and simply observe. Use an intention such as: "I am open to learning from this patch of soil. I am consciously exploring this small section of earth."

Tune in to the smell, texture, and sight of the soil. What organisms do you see? What colors do you observe? What is the texture? Is it moist, dry, or somewhere in between? There is a busy, intricate world here. Some of the organisms might be visible, but many are not.

Sit and hold the awareness that there is an invisible active world in this small space of soil. Record any insights in your journal.

Exploration
COMPOST ALCHEMY

Type of Exploration: Elemental

Supplies Needed:
- Compost bin or container
- Raw materials for compost
- Journal or paper
- Pen or pencil

Ideal Setting: A space in your yard or on your patio or porch where you have room for a compost bin

Child Friendly: Yes

Compost is decayed organic matter. When we walk in a forest, we can observe a natural composting process taking place. Decaying tree leaves and animal droppings work together to create humus, the organic part of soil that nourishes new plants. How brilliant of the earth to create this cycle of death and rebirth! When we create compost in our gardens we are co-creating, working with the natural process of plants decomposing.

Alchemy is the process of turning mundane materials into something valuable. In medieval times, the focus was on creating gold or an elixir of immortality. The transformation of waste material into compost is a kind of alchemy. We start with garbage and we end with a product that enriches our soil, nourishes our plants, and—as a bonus—reduces the amount of garbage going to landfills.

Creating compost is a long-term commitment, but it's also a great way to engage in a mindful connection to the world every day. You'll first need to consider if you have the space to compost. There are now many small compost tumblers and containers that can fit on a patio or in a small backyard, making composting accessible to more people.

Composting involves three basic ingredients:

- Carbon, found in dried leaves and twigs (considered the browns)
- Nitrogen, found in vegetable and fruit scraps, coffee grounds, and grass clippings (considered the greens)
- Water, because moisture is needed to help break down the organic materials

Compost tumblers make it easy to turn and mix a compost pile, which helps the compost break down quicker. Tumblers also keep critters away. Do not add meat scraps, vegetable oil, or dog and cat waste. Meat may attract unwanted animals like rodents and raccoons. Remember that even if they can't get into the tumbler, they will show up and try. If the compost pile does not heat up enough, meat may also provide a host for unhealthy bacteria. Vegetable oil slows down the process. The waste of any carnivorous animal, including dogs and cats, may contain parasites and harmful microorganisms that cannot be killed off without sufficient heat.

In *Mike McGrath's Book of Compost,* author Mike McGrath recommends aiming for four parts of the browns with one part of the greens. He explains that "the dry brown shredded leaves come into the picture teeming with microbes; the wet green, nitrogen-rich material is food for those microbes. When they get together, things get hot, and you get compost."[9]

Many local organic gardening clubs offer free or low-cost composting workshops. You can also find a lot of information online about how to get started.

You may be asking yourself right now what all this has to do with mindfulness. Obviously, someone could choose to make compost in a distracted and unfocused way. But composting, if we choose to do it, provides a way for us to tune in to the earth on a regular basis. We can intentionally focus on the alchemical and magical nature of this process.

~~~~~~~~~

The entire process of composting can be a ritual of awareness, from walking to the compost bin with our organic scraps to turning the bins. Give thanks to your organic material and the cycle of life it represents. Find an affirmation that resonates with you as you add material. Here are some to get started, but feel free to write your own: "I am grateful for compost and its role in the cycle of life. I am co-creating rich nutrients for my garden. I am thankful to these plants that will enrich the soil and create new life."

When the compost is "cooked" and we are ready to welcome the finished product to our garden, we can create a mini ritual for that as well. Composting equals alchemy.

Capture any insights about composting in your journal on a regular basis.

Exploration
SENSING AIR

Type of Exploration: Elemental and movement

Supplies Needed:
- Journal or paper
- Pen or pencil

---

9. McGrath, *Book of Compost,* 11.

Ideal Setting: A garden or other green space

Child Friendly: Yes

Air is obviously a very different element than earth. Earth feels solid beneath our feet and can be touched and held. Air is invisible and yet we are enfolded in it. We often forget that it is all around us. This first activity is a meditation and observation of air. Begin with an intention such as: "I am consciously attuning to air energy. I am open to sensing and learning from this energy."

Air is crucial to our life on the planet, so we begin with breath. Sitting or standing in the garden, bring your attention to your breathing. Let the air come in and out gently through your nose. Take a few minutes to just be present with the garden and your breath.

When you are ready, move your attention to the invisible atmosphere around you. Notice the feeling of air on your face, hands, arms, and any other skin that is exposed. If it is not a windy day, the touch of the atmosphere on your skin may be almost imperceptible. Stay with it.

Next, focus on your arms. Begin to move them slowly up and down in front of your body. As you do this, sense the gentle resistance. We are so used to this resistance that we are often not aware of it. It may help to close your eyes as you are moving your arms. With eyes closed, you may want to visualize the air as having a noticeable color.

Open your eyes and begin to walk slowly through the garden. Focus on feeling the resistance of air as you move. Try this activity for a minimum of ten minutes. Record any insights in your journal.

Exploration
MAKING AIR VISIBLE

Type of Exploration: Elemental

Supplies Needed:
- Journal or paper
- Pen or pencil
- Materials that move in the wind, such as ribbons, flags, and wind-chimes (optional)

Ideal Setting: A garden or other green space

Child Friendly: Yes

Air moves things. That is easy to observe on a windy day, but on calm days, it is easy to forget. We can tune in to air by watching the movement it creates. Sit or stand in the garden and take a few minutes to become quiet and centered. Then begin to watch plants that are being moved by the air. Observe the whole garden at first. Movements might be dramatic or they might be more subtle, but the air is always flowing. The movements will shift and change as you watch.

Next, let your focus go to one particular plant and just observe the rhythmical sway created by air. The sun is heating the air. Hot air rises, cool air sinks, and it all begins to flow, creating air currents. Tune in to the awareness of ever-changing air currents. We can't see them, but they are very real. Hold this focus for at least ten minutes. Record any insights in your journal.

An Added Dimension to Making Air Visible

If you have your own greenspace, increase your awareness of movement by adding windchimes, flags, ribbons, or anything that moves with the wind. Then when you are in the garden, the movement will call your attention to the air. When you notice the movement, acknowledge the dance of energy and imperceptible changes that are taking place each moment. Record any insights in your journal.

My yard has movement and color year-round because I have added ribbons, prayer flags, and origami cranes. I hang strings of origami cranes from trees and trellises, where they dance in the wind. You don't have to spend a lot of money on garden decorations; my cranes are made out of paper, but they have been amazingly resilient to the Denver sun, hail, snow, and wind, and they usually last at least twelve months.

Within the Buddhist tradition, prayer flags are printed with prayers that are carried out to the universe as the flags flap in the wind. I respectfully borrow that good idea of sending intentions out into the world when I decorate my garden. As I fold and string my origami cranes, I focus on an intention for peace and harmony.

Exploration
SENSING FIRE AS LIGHT

Type of Exploration: Elemental

Supplies Needed:
- Journal or paper
- Pen or pencil

Ideal Setting: A garden or other green space

Child Friendly: Yes

The element of fire has aspects of both heat and light. The sun, our burning star, provides both and is the ultimate symbol of this element. We can explore this element's effects in our gardens by focusing on each of these aspects in turn. This first exploration is about light.

One of the easiest ways to experience the sun safely and dramatically in the garden is at dawn and dusk. The play of colors, light, and shadows shift rapidly at those times. Ideally, committing at least forty-five minutes to this activity will allow you to observe significant changes. Begin about fifteen minutes before sunrise or sunset. If possible, turn off any outdoor lights that might interfere with your observation of the garden.

Find a place to sit or stand to observe the garden. Breathe and center yourself. Begin with an intention: "I am consciously attuning to the fire energy of light. I am open to sensing and learning from this energy."

Scan the garden and pay close attention to the light and colors. Let your eyes be drawn to a specific plant or group of plants and stay with them to notice the changing light. We can't feel it, but the planet is moving as we sit and watch. Be aware that what you are observing is happening because our planet is turning on its axis, with our location either turning toward the sun or away. Most of us have probably known that fact since elementary school, but how often do we consider it? We can shift our awareness from knowing this as a fact in our heads to embracing the wonder of this process. Once the sun makes its appearance or disappearance, continue to observe as the light and dark interact and one becomes dominant. Be present with this flowing visual energy. Record any insights in your journal.

Lunar Variations

This activity is interesting to do at the full moon and new moon. The full moon will rise as the sun sets, and once it clears any houses, it will shine its reflected light on the garden. The full moon has a muted brightness, creating a different perspective of softened colors and moon shadows.

At the new moon, the evening will be darkest once the sun goes down. If there are no artificial lights, you will be able to observe as colors and shapes almost completely fade from view. Experiencing the difference between the two allows us to consciously tune in to this rhythm of the sun, moon, and earth that is constantly taking place.

Record any insights in your journal. What did you notice about light emerging and fading? How do colors change as the light shifts?

Exploration
SENSING FIRE AS WARMTH AND HEAT

Type of Exploration: Elemental

Supplies Needed:
- Journal or paper
- Pen or pencil

Ideal Setting: A garden or other green space where you can stay for an entire day or several hours. It is recommended to do this activity in the summertime during the cooler morning hours before midday.

Child Friendly: Yes

This activity is an observation of warmth and heat in the garden. It's best done throughout the day or at least over a few hours so that you can observe changes in the garden.

Warmth is important to most plants. Too much can scorch or kill plants; too little, and plants won't thrive. Most gardeners pay attention to heat and warmth, especially with tender plants. Depending on where you live, there are different concerns. In my Pennsylvania garden, I often worried there was not enough warmth for heat-loving plants like eggplants and tomatoes. In my Denver garden, the heat can be so intense at midday that I cover plants with shade cloth, a fabric that reduces the amount of heat getting through.

Plants can't seek shade as humans do, so they have developed a number of strategies to protect themselves—when possible—from intense heat. Leaves fold in on themselves and droop to reduce their surface area. If it's too hot, some plants will give up and begin to quickly go to seed to ensure a next generation. Lettuce and other greens will bolt in hot weather; they send up a stalk with flowers, then seeds.

~~~~~

Begin this exploration with an intention: "I am consciously attuning to the fire energy of heat. I am open to sensing and learning from this energy." Start this exploration in the morning when it is still cool outside. Get an overall feel for the garden, walking through and observing plants. Identify the plants you want to check in with throughout the day. You may want to make a quick sketch to help you with your observations.

Once you are familiar with the garden, make a point of observing the plants every hour. What do you notice that's different? How are they responding to the sun? Do they appear happy or stressed? Do they seem to want or need more heat or less? This activity calls our attention to balance. Like many things in life, there is a tipping point between optimal and detrimental. Record any insights in your journal.

Exploration
MAKING FIRE VISIBLE

Type of Exploration: Elemental

Supplies Needed:
- Journal or paper
- Pen or pencil

Ideal Setting: A garden or other green space

Child Friendly: Yes

We can call our attention to the fire element by adding items to our green space that catch and reflect light. Gazing balls and prisms that create rainbows can be nice additions. If you place prisms by a street, be sure they are not hung where they will reflect light into the eyes of drivers. Other ornaments that catch and shimmer can look beautiful in a garden. You could also introduce a sundial that tracks the progress of the sun across the sky. Any of these add beauty and interest to the garden, and that might be enough. But you can use them in an intentional way—when they catch your eye because of the sun, call yourself back to the present moment. Let these items serve as a reminder to be present in this space.

Exploration
SENSING WATER

Type of Exploration: Elemental

Supplies Needed:
- Journal or paper
- Pen or pencil

Ideal Setting: A garden or other green space early in the morning

Child Friendly: Yes

Water, like the other three elements, makes life possible on the planet. It also has some quirky attributes. Unlike most other substances, water expands rather than contracts when it freezes. This makes the solid form of water lighter than the liquid form. Ice floats on water and allows lakes, ponds, and rivers to freeze on the surface. Plants, fish, and other sea creatures remain alive below the ice. This remarkable trait enabled life to form on Earth.

This first activity is about tuning in more fully to water in the garden. If you live in a place where dew forms (which is most places, unless it is extremely dry), that can be a great starting point. Water is a shape-shifter and changes from a gas (water vapor) to a liquid (dew) when conditions are right for water to condense onto plants. Early in the morning is the best time to observe dew.

~~~~~~~

Begin with an intention: "I am consciously attuning to water energy in the garden. I am open to sensing and learning from this energy."

Sit, stand, or walk slowly through the garden. If dew has formed, you may want to walk barefoot to tune in to this energy. What does it feel like to have dew on your skin?

Bring your attention to other forms of water in the garden. There may be a sprinkler system or other irrigation that allows you to observe the flow of water to plants. Even if there is not a visible flow of water, know that every green plant you see is made up of a significant portion of water. Water is flowing through plants, transporting nutrients, keeping them healthy and hydrated.

Humans also are made up of a significant amount of water. Like the plants, water transports nutrients within humans and keeps us healthy. Sense your connectedness to plants and to water. Record any insights in your journal.

Exploration
EXPERIENCING GARDEN RAIN

Type of Exploration: Elemental

Supplies Needed:
- Journal or paper
- Pen or pencil

Ideal Setting: A garden or other green space during a gentle rain

Child Friendly: Yes

This activity requires waiting for the right condition, a gentle rainstorm, so that you can immerse yourself in rain as plants in the garden might. Plan to head outside the next time it is raining, but don't go out in a lightning storm!

State an intention as you go out: "I am consciously connecting with the rain falling on this garden." Then stand and allow yourself to feel the rain on your face and any exposed skin. Be present with this amazing process. Through evaporation and transpiration (from leaves), water has traveled as vapor up to the clouds and now is falling back to earth, where you and the garden are recipients. You are receiving this gift. Be aware of how unique this cycle of events is. Humans do not know of any other planets where this is happening.

Bring your awareness to the garden and the plants around you. Imagine for a moment that you are one of the garden plants receiving this rejuvenating and refreshing water from the sky. You are all sharing in this event together.

Record any insights in your journal. What did you discover? How would you describe the experience of rain?

Going Deeper with Elemental Archetypes

Each of the elements—earth, air, fire, and water—resonate with deeper meanings than their obvious functions in the garden. This is where the fifth element, spirit, comes in. As sentient beings, we embody this fifth element. We interact with the elements, recognizing their functions and their mythic power and poetry.

Earth has a resonance for all the things that nourish, protect, sustain, and heal us. Air vibrates with inspiration, intuition, intellect, and all the unseen things that move us. Fire encompasses the idea of purification, creativity, change, transformation, and rising from the ashes. Water encompasses fluidity, flexibility, flowing emotions, the unconscious, and shape-shifting.

Each element also has plants that correspond to it. Deeply rooted plants like comfrey, dandelion, and burdock carry a lot of earth energy. Plants that vibrate with the energy of air are easily moved by air or have scent carried easily on the wind. These include yarrow, fennel, anise, and amaranth. Garlic, mustard, onion, arugula, and other strong, spicy plants belong to fire. Water plants include willow, water lily, fern, and moss.

If you find the idea of elements helpful in navigating the world, working with them simply requires your mindful attention. Stating an intention to work with the elements or one particular element is one way to begin. Working with the elements is a way to mindfully connect with the kaleidoscope of stimuli in the world. You can create ways to be more attentive to noticing patterns and connections.

One basic way to do this is through journaling. Writing helps you be more attentive as you observe because you know you'll be recording it. Keeping a journal is also a kind of commitment. If you decide to record your observations about elemental connections, there is more likelihood that you will remember to do that during the day.

Creating an altar, either indoors or out, is another activity that can focus your attention. An altar can be as simple as placing a favorite stone (earth), a sprig of yarrow (air), some mustard seeds (fire), and a small bowl filled with water in a visible location. You can, of course, create something much more elaborate—whatever is to your liking. The point is that an altar will keep your attention on your stated goal of connecting with the garden elements.

You can plant your gardens by paying special attention to the elements, choosing plants that are connected to each. Including elemental plants in your diet is another way to invite a deeper connection or understanding of specific elements. (Please do research first to be sure they are edible.) I often reach for dandelion root tea when I am feeling off balance and in need of grounding earth energy. I drink Tulsi (holy basil) when I need inspiration, and garlic is my go-to fire element food.

Exploring the elements as they relate to the garden and to mindfulness can be an ongoing process of discovery.

Creating Your Own Elemental Map of the Garden

The four elements are one way to view the world. They are a map, and "the map is not the territory."[10] There are other maps. Within traditional Chinese medicine, there is a five-element map of the world. The elements in that map are wood, fire, earth, metal, and water. Don't get hung up on which elemental map is correct; they are just different ways to frame an understanding of the energies in the world.

You could, as an experiment, attempt to define your own personal garden energies. I love the quartet of earth, air, fire, and water, so I have not been moved to look for other elements, although I do think it could be an interesting project.

If it is something you are drawn to, it would involve devoting time to meditating in the garden, being open to inspiration and guidance, and tuning in to your creative self to find something new. Art can sometimes help us discover things quicker than words can. Grab some markers and poster board, sit in the garden, and simply observe. What energies do you notice? What categories do

10. Korzybski, *Science and Sanity*, vii.

the energies fall into? Are they garden-specific energies, or do they exist universally? How are they connected? What are their traits? Can you name them?

Many moons ago, other sentient beings contemplated the world and created the elemental maps we have now. If we observe the world as it constantly bubbles up into form, we can create our own maps that reflect our unique understanding of the world.

five

EXPLORATIONS OF CONNECTEDNESS

Activities in this section enhance the awareness of connectedness between ourselves and the green world. You could make a case that any mindfulness practice is about connecting, but the explorations in this section have connectedness as their primary focus.

The first two meditations are some of my favorites, especially early in the morning or at dusk, when the world is a little quieter. They are contemplative in nature and require you to simply be present and sense your moment-by-moment connection to the world. They are introduced here as sitting or standing practices, but they could be incorporated into a walking meditation as well.

Exploration
MEDITATION IN THE GARDEN

Type of Exploration: Deepening awareness

Supplies Needed:
- Comfortable clothes
- Chair, meditation cushion, or blanket to sit on
- Journal or paper

- Pen or pencil
- Timer (optional)

Ideal Setting: A garden or green space where you feel comfortable meditating

Child Friendly: Yes

If you have a regular sitting or standing meditation practice, move it outdoors. Work with your journal on this one. What do you discover in moving your practice outdoors? What do you notice that is the same? What do you notice that is different?

If you are new to meditation, what follows is a simple green world meditation. Find a place to sit or stand in the garden or outdoor space. You can close your eyes if you choose, but this meditation is good to do with your eyes open.

Helpful meditation posture involves being alert but relaxed, sitting or standing in a way that enables you to take a full breath. Whether sitting or standing, imagine you are a marionette with a string at your crown that is gently pulling your head up. Your back should be straight but not rigid; keep your tailbone pointing down. Check that your jaw and shoulders are relaxed.

Many mindfulness practices begin with the breath. The breath provides an easy pathway, as it is always with us and connects us to life and the rest of the world. It is also free and easily accessible. As you breathe in slowly, feel the air running past your nostrils to the back of your throat and your lungs. Let your diaphragm expand as the air flows into your lungs.

Count slowly to determine the length of your inhale. Then increase the count of your exhale by two. For example, if your inhale is six counts, then exhale to eight. If the count of your inhale is five, then exhale to seven. Remain focused on your breathing for ten complete cycles. Don't skip the beginning breaths—they signal to our brains that we are shifting into a calming activity.

Now begin to move your awareness to the garden space around you. As you breathe in, be aware that the air flowing into you was touching the plants in your field of vision just moments before. Feel air and energy from nearby plants entering your lungs. As you breathe out, know that the air is returning to the plants around you. If your mind wanders, you can work with an intention: "I am here in the garden breathing in. I am here in the garden breathing out."

With each inhale, focus on a place close to you in the garden that you feel the oxygen and energy are being pulled from. As you exhale, allow the energy to flow back to that place. As you continue to practice, slowly expand the reach of your breath as far as you can see until you are energetically breathing in and out from the farthest point. Sit or stand and continue to breathe in and out.

Continue for at least ten minutes. Set a timer if you'd like; otherwise, meditate as long as you feel is right for you. When you are ready to wrap things up, bring your attention and breath back to the garden space around you for the last few breaths of the meditation.

Record your thoughts in your journal. How did your connection to the garden shift or change? What did you discover?

Exploration
GARDEN IMMERSION

Type of Exploration: Deepening awareness

Supplies Needed:
- Comfortable clothes
- Chair, meditation cushion, or blanket to sit on
- Journal or paper
- Pen or pencil
- Timer (optional)

Ideal Setting: A garden where you feel comfortable meditating

Child Friendly: Yes

In this energetic awareness practice, we use breath and imagery to experience our rhythmic connection with the green world. We begin with our senses, focusing on each one in series, but then move beyond them.

Sitting or standing in the green space, begin with the grounding and opening breaths.

Feel or imagine that your sight and breathing are intimately connected. As you breathe through your nostrils you are also breathing in through your eyes. Imagine the colors, shapes, and energies flowing toward you and entering your eyes on the inhale. Feel the fluidness of the natural world and the garden. On the exhale, allow the energy to flow back out to the garden. Be as present as you can to this flowing of energy back and forth, like waves coming onto the shore and then receding. Continue for at least six breaths.

Gently refocus your attention on hearing and sound energy. Allow the energies of sound to flow toward you and into you. Imagine that you can feel the sound waves coming from all parts of the garden into your ears and your being, then imagine them flowing out again.

Continue for at least six breaths.

Gently refocus your attention on fragrance and smell. If it is summer where you are, you might experience more dramatic sensations, but this exploration can be done any time with more subtlety. As you inhale, imagine the fragrance of the garden flowing into every cell of your body. Continue for at least six breaths.

For a final time, gently refocus and direct your attention to absorbing the whole experience. We are aiming for a gestalt experience here, which means a whole that is bigger than the sum of its parts. You are immersing yourself in this space. With each inhale, waves of energy from the garden are flowing to you and through you. Waves of energy are not only entering through your nose, mouth, eyes, and ears, but also through your pores and skin.

Imagine and feel, if you can, the energy of this place touching you and integrating into your being. As you continue to breathe, feel the gentle rhythm of your breaths in and out as waves melting into you. Embrace being fully present in this rhythmical flow of energy. Continue for at least six breaths.

When you are ready to close the meditation, allow your awareness of waves of energy to fade into the background. Bring your awareness back to the breath entering and exiting your nose. Take five or six breaths with this focus and then close.

Record your thoughts in your journal. How did the meditation shift your awareness of the garden? What did you experience? What did you discover? How is this different from your usual meditation practice?

Exploration
BECOMING A PLANT

Type of Exploration: Deepening awareness and contemplation

Supplies Needed:
- Journal or paper
- Pen or pencil

Ideal Setting: A garden or other green space

Child Friendly: Yes, recommended for ages eight and up

This meditation is about exploring life from a plant perspective, as much as we are able.

Find a plant in your green space that you can comfortably sit with. Begin with opening and centering breaths, then observe your plant for a few minutes. Explore the plant by sight and smell. If it is not a bristly or stinging plant, gently run your hands along the stem. Explore the leaves, branches, buds, and flowers.

What is the energy of this plant? Is it tall or low to the ground? How might height affect the plant? Does it have to reach up for sunlight? Are there other plants close by? What seems to be its relationship with other plants? Do other plants shade it, provide cover, or take needed nutrients from your plant, or are they supporting each other in some way?

As you sit with this plant, imagine what it would be like to be this plant. You can close your eyes or leave them open—whatever will help you tune in to this experience. Allow yourself to embody this plant as much as possible. Imagine your roots sinking into the ground, searching for moisture and nutrients. Your roots also hold you here in this place. There is nowhere to go. Your life takes place right here. Your limbs might stretch out in different directions, but your roots keep you anchored.

Imagine the feel of the wind on your leaves and the difference between a light breeze and a fierce storm. Take time with each. Next, imagine a gentle rain on your leaves and the difference between that and a hailstorm. Lastly, consider the feel of sunshine. Imagine first the morning sun that touches the leaves. Then imagine the sun at high noon during summertime; it may be hot and uncomfortable. Whatever the weather, your plant will be remaining right here and making any adjustments it can, like curling or drooping leaves, a kind of hunkering down. How does it feel to simply be immersed in the elements, for better or worse?

Are there flowers on your plant? Flowers are the sexual organs of plants, and the exchange of pollen creates seeds for a next generation. Plants rely on pollinators (in most cases) to move their pollen out to other plants. Are there pollinators visiting your flowers and creating new life? What is that experience like?

How does it feel to not use words for communication? How else might you communicate? What does your life force and energy field feel like? Are you aware of projecting it out into the space around you? Is there a color to it, or a shape? Are you aware of the energy fields of the plants around you?

Let the plant you have chosen be your guide. What else are you aware of about how this plant exists and how it experiences the world?

When you are ready, bring your attention back to your breath and your own experience of the world. Record any discoveries or insights in your journal. How has your awareness of this plant shifted?

Exploration
BECOMING A TREE

Type of Exploration: Deepening awareness and contemplation

Supplies Needed:
- A tree to work with
- Journal or paper
- Pen or pencil

Ideal Setting: A garden, park, or green space where you feel comfortable meditating

Child Friendly: Yes, recommended for ages eight and up

This meditation follows a similar pattern to the previous one. However, trees have different energy than garden plants, making these two distinct meditations. Trees are, of course, larger than most garden plants, and they have more noticeable effects on humans. They provide shade and act as windbreaks.

They create habitats for birds and other city creatures. Many trees live as long as humans or even longer. They are huge living entities that we share space with, yet we often walk right by without noticing them. This meditation is a starting point for being more mindful of their living presence.

~~~~~

Begin by selecting a tree you want to work with. If it is a tree in a public place, make sure you'll feel comfortable sitting by the tree to do this meditation.

When you are ready, start with opening breaths and centering yourself. Then explore the tree by sight and smell. Take the time to check for thorns or sticky sap before touching. Run your hands along the bark and allow yourself to feel its bumps and ridges. Walk around the tree, looking both up and down. Explore the leaves and branches, noting shapes and colors. If there are roots visible above ground, bend down and touch them. Are there other entities living or visiting this tree, like insects, birds, or mammals?

Walk back away from the tree so that you can view it in its entirety. What do you notice stepping back? How do the colors and shape of the tree fit into the landscape? What message or feeling does it hold? You might be able to see the faint glow of the energy field around the tree. Observing from a distance makes it easier to see.

When you are ready, walk back to the tree to begin the meditation. This can be done sitting or standing. Imagine what it would be like to be this tree. Feel first the rootedness. Most trees have roots that extend as far into the ground as the branches extend upward. Imagine what that would feel like, to have roots running from your feet into the planet to hold you safely and firmly in place. Feel also the roots pulling water and nutrients up from the soil toward the trunk.

Imagine the trunk of this tree. The bark creates a solid protective shell. Inside there is a constant flow of activity from the roots to the branches and from the branches back down through the trunk, like many streams of flowing energy. Feel, if you can, the flow of energy up to your branches and leaves as the tree pulls up moisture and nutrients, delivering them to the uppermost branches. Feel also the downward flow as the tree sends food made by the leaves back down to the branches, trunk, and roots.

Be aware of the exchange of energy with the surrounding air. Water transpires from your leaves, heading off into the clouds. Sunlight touches your leaves, making food which is sent back down through the branches and trunk.

Next, take time to sense your immersion in the elements. Imagine the feel of the wind and the difference between a soft breeze and a powerful storm. Consider the rain on your tree, both a gentle rain and a harsh rain or hail. Focus on the feel of sunshine and the difference between warm sunshine that is just right and the sometimes-too-hot sun of summer. Whatever the weather, this tree will be standing in it. The upper and outer leaves and branches will experience the weather more intensely. How does it feel to simply be immersed in the elements rather than being able to walk away?

Consider the fact that you have no words for communication. How else might you communicate? What is your relationship to other trees and plans around you? Let the tree you have chosen be your guide. What else are you aware of about how this tree exists and experiences the world?

When you are ready, bring your attention back to your breath and your own experience of the world. In your journal, record any discoveries and insights. What did you discover about this tree and your perceptions of it? If you did both the garden plant meditation and the tree meditation, what differences and similarities between the two did you discover?

Exploration
CONTEMPLATING PHOTOSYNTHESIS

Type of Exploration: Deepening awareness and contemplation

Supplies Needed:
- Journal or paper
- Pen or pencil

Ideal Setting: A garden or green space where you feel comfortable meditating

Child Friendly: Yes, recommended for ages eight and up

Plants make human life on our planet possible. Photosynthesis, the process plants engage in to create their own food, provides us with both food and oxygen. Most of us learned this in elementary school, but it is a fact we often tuck away without reflecting on how remarkable it is. We can explore a deeper mindful connection with plants and trees by considering photosynthesis.

Green plants have chloroplasts, specialized parts of cells that enable them to create their own food, and in turn create all the food on earth. (Humans either eat plants directly or eat animals that have consumed plants.) Sunlight touching leaves initiates the process. Carbon dioxide is a key ingredient in this process. As plants use the carbon dioxide, they release oxygen as a waste product.

In this mindfulness practice, we'll focus on this process, first directing our attention to the food-making ability of green plants and then the oxygen generation.

~~~~~~~

To begin, find a tree or plant you'd like to work with. This can be done as an extension of the previous tree or plant meditations or as a stand-alone practice. A tree produces more oxygen than a smaller garden plant, but you can do this practice with any plant. We are not measuring the amount of food and oxygen produced, but cultivating an awareness of this exchange that happens all over the planet.

When you are ready, become centered with opening breaths. Bring your attention to the leaves of the plant or tree. Consider how plants can create their own food with water, carbon dioxide, and sunlight. This is in stark contrast to humans; we must find and ingest food to keep ourselves nourished. Imagine simply holding your arms out in the sun and being able to create the food you need to survive. This living being in front of you sustains itself without kitchens, appliances, restaurants, or farmers markets. Sit with this realization for a few minutes. What would it feel like to be able to create food in your body as the sun shone on you?

Now shift your awareness to your breath. We breathe in oxygen and exhale carbon dioxide. Plants use carbon dioxide for photosynthesis and then release oxygen. Be aware that trees and plants are supporting our existence on the planet. We, in turn, are helping support the green world's existence.

Concentrate on the exchange of energy. Energy is coming from the tree and flowing into your nostrils and lungs. Your body takes the parts that it needs and sends out carbon dioxide. On your exhale, imagine the carbon dioxide flowing out and being gathered in by this plant and others. Feel this flowing of energy like waves moving on and off shore.

Now imagine that you and the tree are not separate from each other, but are part of one being. You are connected by the ground beneath your feet and the atmosphere around you. Within this being is a flow of energy back and forth. It's a gentle rhythm of aliveness as we each take what we need and share what we don't with the other.

Stay with this practice *at least* ten minutes. See if you can carry this awareness of our vital connection to plants into your day with you. In your journal, record discoveries and insights.

Shinrin-Yoku: Into the Woods

My earliest memories of forests are the fuzzy images of the trees behind my childhood home. Our backyard property line shifted into a deeply wooded area, or at least that is how it looked through my five-year-old eyes. I remember helping my mother gather violets among the trees. It seemed mysterious and a little spooky. I realize now it wasn't much of a forest, just the last remnants of a once-wild area that would soon be cut down for new homes.

There were many trees in our neighborhood, spread out on various lots. My favorite was an old weeping willow which all the neighborhood kids loved to climb. Some daredevils would go much higher than me, but I was happy getting myself to the first crook of its huge branches. They opened like a crow's nest on a ship where one could sit and look out at the world. The tree felt ancient, and together with a sister willow they were some of the oldest trees on our block. Someone had the good sense to let them be when they were constructing houses on our block.

My next experience with tree elders occurred in tenth grade. Our botany teacher sent us to gather leaves at the Erie Cemetery. The cemetery, located in the heart of the city, had some of the oldest and most diverse groupings of trees. As teenagers, my friends and I were a little creeped out to be assigned a cemetery field trip. However, once there, we were impressed by the beauty and immensity of some of the trees. We discovered oak, tulip, black walnut, pine, maple, and more. They weren't just examples of trees from our textbook; they were vibrant, huge beings each with a distinct energy and personality, many of them towering eighty feet or more above us.

As a young city dweller, I didn't have many opportunities to be in a forest. My interaction with trees was often one-on-one. In our own yard, my father had apple trees and a large black walnut, each with their own distinct energy. I can still close my eyes and visualize those trees and their fragrance.

My family didn't go to the woods, but we spent a lot of time at the beach. Presque Isle State Park is a peninsula that juts into Lake Erie. There are miles of beaches, many of them lined by cottonwoods and willows. The cottonwoods have a sweet and earthy smell in the spring, especially when wet. They created a backdrop and ambiance for the park experience, but they didn't make a forest.

When I was married and in my early twenties, we began taking occasional camping trips in the Allegheny National Forest. That shifted my awareness about the woods. There is a different energy to a community of trees in a forest. The density of trees creates a critical mass and a feeling of being in a protective bubble, a respite from urban activities.

I didn't realize it at the time, but the Allegheny National Forest does not have many old trees. Most of the original trees were cut down by loggers by the early 1900s. When I finally had the opportunity to visit old growth forests in Montana and California, it was like entering a temple. Most visitors automatically speak in whispers, much like they would in any sacred space. The energy and presence of these giant beings is palpable. Being in the woods can be an awe-inspiring and feel-good experience.

Feeling good in the woods is now supported by research.[11] Simply by spending time in the forest, the body becomes more resilient. Shinrin-yoku, or forest bathing, grew out of the research. This is "the practice of walking slowly through the woods, in no hurry, for a morning, an afternoon or a day."[12]

A two-hour walk in the woods has numerous health benefits. Research is ongoing, but some studies reveal that the increased oxygen and the natural oils released by trees play a part in the health benefits.[13]

Japan has embraced this idea. They have identified sixty-two healing forests and provide information to their citizens about the features of each. At some

---

11. Li, *Forest Bathing*, 63–68.
12. Miyazaki, *Shinrin Yoku*, 10.
13. Li, *Forest Bathing*, 38–39.

locations, there are even specialists available to help people commune with the forest.[14]

Spending time in the woods has a definite measurable effect on our health. Being in the woods, like being in a garden, can be a doorway to mindfulness, but mindfulness involves intention. We could walk in the woods while talking with a friend or read a book under a tree. Those are wonderful and healthy activities, but they do not embody the practice of mindfulness. I've also observed people walking on wooded paths while talking on cell phones. Others are so intent on documenting their hike by taking photos that they are not actually present.

The forest, like the garden, can provide an opening to meditation. The lack of distractions, the beauty, and the scents all provide a conducive venue to practice mindfulness. If you have access to a forest, try the connecting activities in this chapter in that setting. Pay attention to any similarities and differences you discover from working in a garden or city green space. Record any insights in your journal.

For most of my life I have not had easy access to the forest, and my mindfulness practice has unfolded in my garden and urban green spaces. Settings are important. Experiment to see what works for you, but don't lose track of the fact that mindfulness is an intentional practice. As we commit to practice, we might be able to tune in to the green world by seeing a dandelion pushing up through the cracks in a city sidewalk just as easily as we can tune in by walking into a forest of a thousand trees.

---

14. Li, *Forest Bathing*, 280.

six

DEEPER EXPLORATIONS

The activities in this section are deeper explorations because they either involve more time or more contemplation. You will also be asked to push your awareness out beyond the garden. This chapter's explorations are similar, in some ways, to part 2 of this book, in which we begin with one plant and its correspondence, then channel that mindful focus into the rest of our lives. Each activity in this section is another way to hone our mindfulness skills.

Please note that deeper explorations are also a matter of perspective. Depending on how you approach the previous chapters, most of the explorations found there could be experienced as deeper dives as well.

Exploration
ALIGNING WITH ONE PLANT

Type of Exploration: Contemplation

Supplies Needed:
- Journal or paper (Consider a dedicated journal for this practice)
- Pen or pencil

Ideal Setting: A garden or other green space

Child Friendly: Yes

Choosing one plant as a mindfulness anchor can have a profound effect on our awareness and powers of observation. I discovered this by accident in my early days of working with herbs. I had been reading about *Echinacea* (commonly known as coneflower) and wanted to include it in my garden. I ordered some seeds from a mail-order company, but I didn't actually know what *Echinacea* looked like. This may be hard to imagine, but it was pre-internet! It was before *Echinacea* became a poster child for herbal remedies. It was also a time when a lot of seed catalogs—especially those for nontraditional plants—were basically a black-and-white printed list with a few drawings.

When the seeds arrived, I started them in pots inside my house to get an early start and to be sure of their identity once transplanted. I hovered over these plants every day, watching every minute sign of growth. Once they were planted in the garden, I visited the plants as often as I could to check on their progress. I also dragged various family members out of the house to observe the plants with me, although they were not as excited about this as I was. I wasn't drawing plants at this time, as described in chapter 1, but I think if someone had asked me to draw the plants from memory, I could have done it. It was my summer keenly observing *Echinacea*.

Many perennials need to get established before they will flower, so I was prepared for no flowers the first year. However, by midsummer, buds started to form. This was exciting for me, but not so much for my family, as I was reenergized in forcing them out to the garden to see this phenomenon. As the buds slowly opened, my excitement shifted to disappointment. It appeared that the plant was just a daisy with pale pink petals and a flat center. I didn't know exactly what *Echinacea* looked like, but I knew there was a cone. I wondered if they sent me the wrong seeds.

Over the next few days I continued my observations. The petal colors darkened and the middle cone became more pronounced. The petals pulled back from the cone. This was indeed *Echinacea*. Every year since, my *Echinacea* has repeated that dance of opening as a pretend daisy and then shifting to its true self once it blossoms.

I learned a lot that summer, and not only about *Echinacea*. Plants change every day just as we do. Cells die and are replaced by others. They make subtle shifts toward the light or water. They may shift because of wind or another plant. Many of us have seen time-lapse photography that shows how a plant moves over a period of hours and days. These minute movements are happening continuously and although we can't always tune in to them, we can observe the differences day-to-day.

～～～～～

When you focus on only one plant, you begin to tune in to subtle changes. You are more likely to see when buds start to form, when leaves begin to change color, and when the plant is thirsty or has had too much sun. This is a rich exercise that can help ground you in the cycles of the seasons and the cycle of death and rebirth.

When selecting a plant to work with, it's important to have easy access to it. You'll want to choose something in your yard or a place you visit often. If you will be doing this practice during the winter months, choose a tree or perennial that will be there for you to work with.

You may already have an affinity for one plant. Maybe it is one of the healing herbs that you've used on a regular basis or a plant you often use in meal preparation. You may notice it in your neighbors' yards when walking down the street. If you don't have an immediate inspiration for the plant you want to work with, walk through your garden or green space with the intention of letting a plant present itself to you.

Once you've identified the plant, create a schedule for when you will do this practice. The practice itself does not have to take a lot of time, but you'll need to return to it on a regular basis. Think about how you will make that happen. If you can do the practice daily, you will tune in to more nuances, but twice a week will work. Find a way to remind yourself of the practice.

On your first visit, take the time to observe the plant and record your impressions. You can begin with some of the opening sensory exercises described in chapter 1. Repeat these activities on different days because you will discover different results. As you continue the practice with this plant, you can also explore some of the craft ideas from chapter 3, like sun prints and leaf rubbings.

Think of each visit as checking in with a friend. Record your observations and insights in your journal. Questions to consider each visit:

- How would you describe this plant to someone who doesn't know it?
- How has it grown or changed since your last entry?
- How has the color or fragrance changed?
- What is the energy of the plant?
- What does it feel like when you are near it?
- What attributes does it have?
- What ideas and concepts does the plant invoke in you?

Take the time to learn about this plant not just from observation, but through the wisdom of others. One of my favorite books for plant history and lore is the two-volume *A Modern Herbal*, first published in 1931 by Maude Grieve. Some of the nutritional and medicinal information is out of date, but the stories about plants and how they have supported humans are fascinating. How does your experience with this plant align with what's been written about it? Are there ways you might integrate this plant into your life in a more intentional way?

This activity works best with a commitment of at least four weeks, but the longer, the better.

Exploration
CONTEMPLATING THE EDGE

Type of Exploration: Contemplation and deepening awareness

Supplies Needed:
- Journal or paper
- Pen or pencil

Ideal Setting: A garden or other green space for observation

Child Friendly: Yes

"The edge" is a permaculture concept. Permaculture is an approach to designing living spaces and gardens with an eye toward sustainability and production. The edge is the place where two distinct environmental systems come together and intermingle. The edge holds more opportunities and interest than one ecosystem. It is richer with diversity and novelty.

The edge will be more dramatic in large systems, like the ocean meeting the shore and the forest melding into the field. But even in a small yard there will be unique microclimates and spaces where they overlap—the edge. Edges occur along the drip lines of trees and the outer areas of a garden bed. They exist in the few feet next to a building that retains heat or an area near a large decorative rock that reflects more light.

Edges stretch the boundaries of what might successfully grow in an area, either with the gardener's intention or as a result of plants discovering their own way to the edge. I have a space at the back of my yard that is partially shaded by a hawthorn tree. It's not a shady or sunny area, but an overlapping area of both. That allows me to comingle sun-loving and shade-loving plants. I have another edge along my patio because the patio absorbs heat, enabling me to plant more tender flowers or herbs there.

It is helpful, when contemplating the edge, to visit a place where the edges are more pronounced, like a stream and bank or a forest and field. Walk along the edge and observe. Notice that the edges along natural systems are wavy patterns, not straight lines. It is usually only humans who try to lay things out in lines and angles. The flowing pattern where natural edges meet increases the surface area of the edge. Take note of the plants and living organisms in this space. Natural edges are not static. How does the edge shift and change? What is the flow between distinct sections?

In your own garden or green space, take time to explore the edges. Walk through your garden while holding the idea of the edge in your awareness. What do you observe?

A key concept in permaculture is optimizing the edge. Where could you take more advantage of the edges? Garden beds with wavy edges mimic natural systems and increase the plant area. Spiral gardens (beds laid out as a spiral mound) create many microclimates so that plants with differing needs can be planted in a close area. The edge along the ground can be optimized by planting upward by using trellises and arbors. Are there ways that you can increase edges or take more advantage of them?

We can also carry the edge concept into our lives. Since we know the edge is more creative, rich, and diverse, how can we think about expanding the edges in our lives? For most of us, there are edges between work time and family time or edges between our book club friends and our workout friends. How might we pay attention to this boundary, stretch it, and increase the richness of those experiences? There are also edges between mornings and afternoons, relaxation time and activity time, waking and sleeping. I have found the edge between waking and sleeping to be particularly creative and insightful. I keep a notebook and pen within easy reach so that I can capture edge ideas as I am drifting off to sleep or just waking.

~~~~~~~~~

Use the edge concept as a subject for contemplation. Sit or walk through your garden or other green space holding the edge as an intentional focus. Large edges will be easier to identify, but smaller edges are everywhere. Hold this concept throughout the day, noticing edges and opportunities in the green world and throughout your life.

What does the idea suggest to you? What are some of the edges in your own life? Are they hard edges or is there a flow to them? What opportunities are available for us in the edges? What are the shapes, colors, and energetic feel to the different edges in your life? Record any insights in your journal.

Exploration
GREEN WORLD SPIRALS

Type of Exploration: Contemplation and deepening awareness

Supplies Needed:
- Journal or paper
- Pen or pencil

Ideal Setting: A garden or other green space for observation

Child Friendly: Yes

The tendrils on my pumpkin plant wrap themselves in spirals around blades of grass and pull themselves up onto the lower branches of the apple tree. The delicate-looking ringlets belie how strong they are. Pole beans, hops, morning glories, and other climbers all use spirals to coil themselves around trellises and poles.

We may not like bindweed, but we can appreciate its ingenuity in employing spirals to attach itself securely to other plants and root itself into the soil like so many corkscrews.

Look closely at a sunflower seed head, a rosebud, a cabbage head, or a pinecone, and you will see spirals. The spiral shape occurs throughout the green world and throughout the universe. There are extremes in spiral size; we find spirals in our DNA and the Milky Way galaxy.

Spirals are symbols of ever-deepening wisdom. They remind us of our potential to move beyond our present understanding of reality. The spiral is also a great analogy for the cycle of the year, which is often presented as a circle where seasons, opportunities, and challenges repeat themselves. Spirals provide a better map of the journey of the cycle of life. Consider gardening; we sow, tend, water, and harvest, but each year is different and deeper. We've learned some things about the plants and our garden, we've improved the soil, and we've gained experience.

As beginning gardeners, we were at the outer edge of the spiral, slowly moving toward the center with each year that passes. I think of my earliest gardening experiences alongside the adults in my life; I loved interacting with plants and having my hands in the soil, but I knew very little. I was on the outer edge of the spiral. Each season of gardening has deepened my understanding.

Our lives follow this pattern as well. We experience loss and gain, grief and joy, friendship and animosity. When we encounter situations for the first time, we can be a bit overwhelmed. As we gain experience and wisdom traveling along the spiral, we aren't knocked to our knees as often by the hard things. We appreciate the good things even more because of our wisdom.

Lessons learned and information we take in are often framed as a linear path, but life is much more of a spiral. Sometimes life presents us with a challenge that we feel like we've faced a hundred times already. We may feel stuck and as if nothing has changed. If we observe carefully, we might discover the same situation, but we are bringing more wisdom and resilience to the game.

The practice of mindfulness itself is like a spiral. We might feel at times that we have ended up in the same place, possibly a place of inattention or struggling to keep our focus. However, if we commit to practice, we move ever more deeply toward the center.

~~~~~~~~

In contemplating the nature of spirals, you can begin by taking note of the spirals in the green world. Sketch them or just notice how often they appear once you are holding them in your awareness. What is the energy of a spiral? How is it different from the energy of a circle? Where do you notice spirals in the garden? Where do you notice the spiral energy in your own life?

Sitting in meditation, you can hold the spiral as the focus of your awareness. Use a visual representation like a sunflower seed head or use your imagination. What insights and discoveries do you have in contemplating spirals?

Record insights in your journal. Where are you noticing spirals in the green world? Where are you noticing spirals in your life?

Exploration
CONTEMPLATING UNITY IN OPPOSITES

Type of Exploration: Contemplation and deepening awareness

Supplies Needed:
- Journal or paper
- Pen or pencil

Ideal Setting: A garden or other green space for observation

Child Friendly: Yes, recommended for ages ten and up

The garden and the world are in a continual dance of opposites. Sometimes two extremes are in sharp contrast, like the coldest days of winter and the peak of summer. Other times opposites weave together, like a hurricane and its calm center. The yin-yang symbol holds the reality of opposites; the circle is half white and half black, but within each color is a tiny dot of the opposite color. The seed of one is held within the other.

This exploration is about being attentive to this phenomenon in the garden and beyond.

Guidelines for Contemplation
What follows are three pairs of opposites for contemplation. Each pair is a reminder of the complexity of the green world. Read over the information for each

pair as a jumping-off point. Then intentionally seek out these concepts and their relationship. This could be a one-time mindfulness exploration or a mindful investigation that lasts many days at a time. As you explore these opposites, you will probably think of your own to investigate.

Begin with the opening breaths, then hold the pair in your awareness as you sit or walk in the garden. As with many mindful explorations, it can be helpful to repeat the words of each pair to let them seep into your awareness and focus your attention.

Where do you notice them and how are they separate and also connected? Move beyond your thoughts about these concepts to energetic feeling. The three pairs of opposites are:

1. Expanding and contracting
2. Light and dark
3. Form and formless

Expanding and Contracting. The pulse of expansion and contraction is a constant garden rhythm. There are sweeping expansions in the spring and summer as plants push out of the ground, leaf out, and flower. Fall and winter reverse the process as plants shed leaves, become smaller, and disappear into the ground. There are also sub-rhythms to this whole process. Peas and salad greens expand quickly in spring and then contract when it gets too hot, just as many plants are expanding. Flowers expand but then contract in midsummer to form seedpods. The seedpods expand in late summer and autumn to release their seeds in various ways. Some burst open like okra. Others, like dandelions, send their seeds sailing on the wind, expanding their range.

There are daily rhythms of expansion and contraction. Leaves open and close their pores during the day to adjust to the heat. Calendula and morning glory flowers open by day and close by night. Nicotiana and moonflowers have a counter-rhythm, opening in the late afternoon and evening and contracting in the morning.

Birds and butterflies expand their wings to fly and contract them to land. Think of rain as expanding the moisture in the garden and dry seasons as contracting it. There is the obvious expansion and contraction of your breath as you meditate. What does the rhythm of expansion and contraction feel like?

Observing at different times of the day and during different seasons will produce different insights and discoveries.

Push this exploration out beyond the garden. Where are the sweeping expansions and contractions in your life right now? Where are the micro expansions and contractions? Are you resisting the rhythm or flowing with it? Record insights and discoveries in your journal.

Light and Dark. The impressionist painter Claude Monet dedicated himself to studying light and shadow. He often painted the same landscape again and again, working to capture the subtle changes of light throughout the day. When we are attentive, we can tune in to these subtle shifts as well, even if we might not be able to capture them on canvas.

There is, of course, an obvious shift between day and night. Start your investigation there and experience the changing of light at dawn and dusk. There are often dramatic changes at this time, especially when the sun first makes its appearance on the horizon and sends out beams of light toward the garden. How do light and dark meet each other in those periods of twilight? Where are the edges of light and dark? What do you observe during this time?

Day and night on their own—not just the transition between the two—provide plenty of opportunities to study light and dark. During the day, begin by noticing the changing shadows and dappling of light, either because of clouds or other plants. Even at noon there will be shadows in the garden. What patterns do you see? How do light and dark shift as the sun moves across the sky? How do plants shift and change their energy in relation to the sunlight? What is the overall feeling of light and dark in the garden?

Depending on the phase of the moon or other background lights, the night garden may still be bathed in light, but it will be softer than sunlight. If possible, turn off any artificial lights in your yard as you do this activity. If it is a full moon, you may be surprised at how much light exists. Most nights, there will be some moonlight reflected in the garden. Take time to let your eyes adjust and be with this semidarkness. How does your awareness of the garden differ from daylight? What is the energy of the garden bathed in moonlight? Where does the moonlight fall and what shadows does it make? How does it shift over time?

The darkness may make the garden feel softer and more mysterious. Not everything is visible, so you must rely more on your other senses. Be aware that the word darkness has some negative connotations in English, yet periods of darkness are vital for many plants' germination and growth. Darkness is also a time of insight, mystery, silence, and rest.

You can push this exploration out beyond the garden by observing the energy of light and dark, and the dance between the two, throughout the day. In your journal, record any insights and discoveries.

Form and Formless. When playing a rhythm, it is the space between the beats that shapes the sound. When using a vase, it is the space inside that makes it functional. In much the same way, the space between plants creates the garden and our experience of it. If a garden was a wall of solid plants, it would be hard to manage and even harder to make sense of.

Shifting your view of space from background to foreground gives you a different picture of the garden. Where is the space and the emptiness in the garden? How does it inform your awareness of the plants and green world?

As gardeners, we know that pruning plants to allow for more space and airflow around them is important, but we don't usually give it more thought than that. We don't often tune in to the space itself. This exploration takes our usual view of the world and flips it. Rather than viewing the plants as foreground, have them move to background. This may take some practice; repeat these words to yourself to help tune in to the concepts: "Substance and emptiness, form and formless."

Perhaps you should start with individual plants rather than the whole garden. What is the space around a particular plant or tree? Is it visible? Is it palpable? Does it have a color? Does it have an energetic footprint or personality? When you are ready, you can shift to taking in more of the garden. Can you rest in awareness of the emptiness around plants? What does that feel like?

Take this idea of form and formless into the rest of your life as well. What happens if you flip your usual way of observing the world and make the formless the foreground? The things you might have highlighted as having substance move to the background. Are your definitions of foreground and background somewhat arbitrary? Use your journal to record any insights and discoveries.

Exploration
BECOMING BACKGROUND

Type of Exploration: Contemplation and deepening awareness

Supplies Needed:
- Journal or paper
- Pen or pencil

Ideal Setting: A garden or other green space

Child Friendly: Yes, recommended for ages ten and up

Western culture's human-centric interpretation of the world emphasizes separateness from the web of life. Humans are viewed as the pinnacle of creation and the rest of the world exists to serve them in some way. When we label the green world as natural capital, it becomes something to use up for personal gain rather than our actual life support system. We might intellectually know these things, but our bias is usually toward separateness and human centeredness.

In this meditation, you will shift your perspective from being the center of all things to being a part of the collective action in the garden. You change from the solitary star of the story to becoming a participant in an unfolding dance. Being attentive and mindful to the collective nature of reality increases your compassion and ability to make healthy decisions for yourself and the planet.

Begin by sitting or standing in your green space and centering with opening breaths. Take enough time to be present with the flow of energy in the garden. (The garden immersion exploration from chapter 5 is a good complement to this one. If you have time, you can begin with that meditation and end with this one.)

When you are ready, shift your awareness to a place that is not centered within you. Imagine you are looking down from above or looking from across the garden as a disinterested observer, simply noticing what is happening. Scan the area to take in the plants and other living organisms. Notice that your human form is just one other organism sharing space with others in this garden. Depending on the time of year, there may be bees, butterflies, birds, squirrels, and other organisms visible to your eye.

Take note of the rhythms and energy of this space. Energy is being exchanged and transformed throughout the area. Plants are changing sunshine into food. Bees are collecting pollen. Birds and squirrels might be looking for food. Within the soil, this same play is being acted out. Insects and organisms are getting on with their lives, each with their own agenda. We are each an organism just like the others, not the star of the story, but one thread in the tapestry.

Practice for at least ten minutes, holding an awareness of this diverse community. When you are ready, consciously bring your attention back to your own body and close with three deep breaths.

In your journal, record your discoveries. What insights did you have? How easy or difficult was it for you to contemplate this larger picture of the garden and your smaller part in it?

A Path Forward

Each of the explorations presented in this chapter are possible ways to approach the green world mindfully. My intention is not to list every possible exploration, but instead to hold up a lantern that will illuminate some of the many paths. There are countless variations and ways to proceed. If you start exploring with the premise that gardens and the green world can be a portal to awareness, you will discover your own pathways.

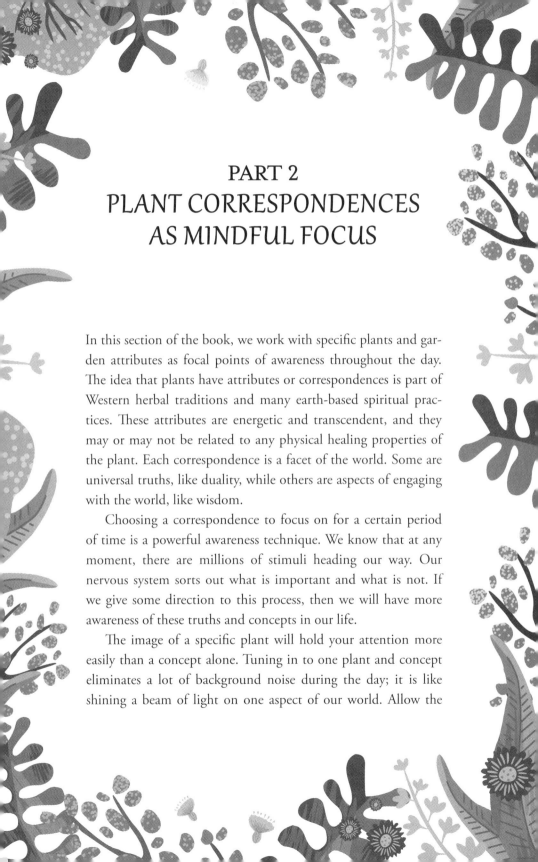

PART 2
PLANT CORRESPONDENCES
AS MINDFUL FOCUS

In this section of the book, we work with specific plants and garden attributes as focal points of awareness throughout the day. The idea that plants have attributes or correspondences is part of Western herbal traditions and many earth-based spiritual practices. These attributes are energetic and transcendent, and they may or may not be related to any physical healing properties of the plant. Each correspondence is a facet of the world. Some are universal truths, like duality, while others are aspects of engaging with the world, like wisdom.

Choosing a correspondence to focus on for a certain period of time is a powerful awareness technique. We know that at any moment, there are millions of stimuli heading our way. Our nervous system sorts out what is important and what is not. If we give some direction to this process, then we will have more awareness of these truths and concepts in our life.

The image of a specific plant will hold your attention more easily than a concept alone. Tuning in to one plant and concept eliminates a lot of background noise during the day; it is like shining a beam of light on one aspect of our world. Allow the experience of this correspondence to provide a focal point for the swirling energies around you.

As we hold the concept in our awareness, we step back to watch what bubbles up. What connections and discoveries do we make when allowing our lives and the world to present themselves through this correspondence?

Each entry in this part of the book provides information and a correspondence for a specific plant. There are fifty-two entries, one for each week of the year. I suggest working with one plant concept a week. The weekly timeframe provides a good balance, allowing enough time to explore a concept while remembering the mind's tendency to want to move on to something new. However, one could easily take any of the concepts and commit to a month- or yearlong exploration of just that correspondence. Begin to train your brain by adopting the weekly practice and, if it feels appropriate, extend it to two weeks, a month, or more.

Although I list one correspondence for each plant, keep in mind that the world is much more complex than that. Many plants share attributes. If another plant, especially one that grows in your own garden, suggests itself for an attribute, go with that one. Having a visual symbol of the correspondence is the point.

You can work with the plants and attributes in the order they are presented, or you can choose a plant and attribute that calls to you each week. This is your journey.

Using Your Journal

Insights and awareness can be fleeting, and the world is a busy place. Using a journal to record your experiences can help you remember and make sense of them. A journal is part of your personal space. Don't worry about grammar or spelling. You can draw pictures, write random words, or write complete sentences—there are no hard rules for capturing your insights. Just remember that this is not primarily an intellectual exercise. You are not simply thinking about a certain plant and attribute, although that can be a part of it; the focus is on your energetic experience. After each entry, there are suggested questions and ideas for shaping your experience. Hold the questions in your awareness and see where they take you.

How to Practice

Working with plants and their correspondences to deepen awareness involves three phases:

1. Attunement
2. Integration
3. Reflection

Generally, attunement is practiced in the morning before you start your day. Integration is practiced throughout the day, and reflection takes place in the evening.

Attunement

Attunement is about establishing a relationship with the plant and correspondence. Once you've chosen a plant and attribute—but before reading the entry—capture in your journal the experience you already have with this plant and attribute. Don't overthink it. Just capture your impressions, but allow enough time to tune in.

If possible, attune outside or with a view of the natural world. Even if this specific plant is not visible in your green space, other plants will vibrate with the same concept. If you can't be outdoors, consider bringing a sprig of the plant indoors or use a picture of the plant to attune with. Questions to consider while attuning:

- What connections do I have with this plant and attribute?
- Where else in the green world do I find this correspondence?
- Describe this attribute in words or draw it energetically. What color is it? What does it feel like? What is the texture? (These may seem like odd questions, but shifting our awareness from words to senses and feelings opens the door to more subtle experiences with the green world and these correspondences. Pose the questions aloud and give space for answers to arise.)
- Is there a place in or around my body or in my life that more strongly resonates with this attribute? (As with the previous question, allow

time and space for answers to percolate.) If you do not feel the attribute, imagine what it would feel like and where you would notice it. Describe that in your journal.

Next, read over that week's entry about the plant and attribute. Each entry will highlight stories or information about a plant and its correspondence. Think of this as opening a doorway to seeing, feeling, and experiencing the connections between the plant, the attribute, and the natural world.

- What resonates for you with the reading?
- How does it influence your awareness of this plant and its correspondence?

Consciously move your awareness to your heart area. What feelings, intuitions, or senses arise as you bring this plant and the concept into your heart awareness?

Sit, stand, or walk in your garden or green space. Hold the concept in your awareness as you breathe. Feel the resonance with the correspondence increasing with each inhale. What do you notice? What are you aware of?

Each morning, reread the information on the plant's correspondence to help realign and attune. All the correspondences are part of the natural world, so we all have connections of one kind or another with each correspondence and plant.

Attunement through Meditation

A morning meditation, holding the plant correspondence in our awareness, will help anchor the mindful focus for the day.

Sitting comfortably, state an intention to connect with this plant and attribute as you begin to meditate. Let the image of the plant and the correspondence wash over you. Think of it as planting an energetic seed in your consciousness and nurturing it each morning. Feel or imagine it resonating with your whole being. Ask yourself if there is a place you feel this attribute in or around your body.

You can also work with an affirmation for each seed concept using the plant and/or attribute to fill in the blanks below.

I am experiencing _____ .

I am aligning with _____ .

I am incorporating _____ into my daily awareness.

Integration

Integration is about gently holding the correspondence and plant in your awareness as you go about your day. One way to practice is by using the breath, repeating the correspondence to yourself with each inhale. Ask yourself periodically during the day where you are noticing this plant or attribute.

Like putting on a pair of tinted glasses, filter the day through this concept. Be attentive to when the plant, attribute, or situations involving them arise. This is not meant to be a mental exploration as much as an experiential. Be aware of the connections and note them. You may be surprised at how often experiences related to the plant or attribute arise.

Our days get busy, so finding ways to remind yourself of the attribute throughout the day is important. Sticky notes are a great tool. You can also use reminders on your phone or tablet, or send scheduled emails to yourself. Bring clippings of the plant indoors or post a photo of the plant in places you'll see it (such as the bathroom mirror). These strategies work well and help us move beyond words.

Another fun way to practice integration for plants that are edible is to include them in meals during the week. Planning recipes around a particular plant, when possible, will keep them at the forefront of your awareness. The idea is to immerse yourself in the plant and its correspondence for a week and observe what happens. Questions to consider for integration:

- In what way is the world reflecting this plant and attribute back to me?
- Where is this plant and/or attribute manifesting in my life?
- What nuances and shades of meaning do I notice with this attribute and plant?

Reflection

Reflection is a powerful method of mindfully reviewing the day. It also helps anchor the energetic attribute in your awareness. Ideally, make time at the end of the day for reflection. This can be as short as one minute, although more time allows for more introspection. When you take time to reflect, it is another way to focus your attention. You stop what you are doing, bring the concept into your awareness, and write or draw your insights.

Identify and try to capture in pictures or words your unique experience with this plant and attribute. Questions to consider when reflecting at the end of the day:

- Where and how did I experience this plant and attribute today?
- How did I embrace this attribute today?
- What insights do I have about this plant or attribute?
- What wisdom does this plant and attribute bring to my life?
- What rings true about this plant's entry and how might I expand it or make it my own?
- What challenges did I have when focusing on this plant and attribute?
- What insights do I have about this plant or attribute?

Week 1
Dandelion and Resilience
Taraxacum officinale

Every child knows the beauty of a field of yellow dandelions and the magic of that field turning to fuzzy seed heads. We can make a wish, blow the seeds away, and hope that they carry our wishes to the ends of the universe. It's odd that so many wishful children grow up to be adults who hate dandelions.

A lot of negative energy is heaped upon dandelions. They are poisoned, mowed over, and reviled constantly. Dandelions regularly appear on labels for toxic weed killers. But dandelions are also one of the most resilient plants. Resilience is the ability to bounce back after adversity, and dandelions exhibit that attribute in abundance.

If you step back from any bias you may have about dandelions, you can probably appreciate all the adaptions it makes to be resilient. First, the dandelion root is a long taproot. If you try to pull it out of the ground and leave even a tiny part of the root, the plant will regenerate. Dandelion seeds take to the wind and spread quickly and for long distances. Dandelions are hardy; they can quickly establish themselves in hostile environments. Another trick the plant employs is morphing from flowers to seeds in less than twenty-four hours. If you pick the flower and leave it on the ground, the flower will close and quickly turn into a seed head. Dandelions can also adapt to the lawn mower by simply growing closer to the ground so that the flowers and seeds develop below the blades.

Interestingly, dandelions also help humans be resilient; dandelions provide a source of free—and almost never-ending—nutritious food. The roots, leaves, and flowers are all edible. The greens can be used like spinach or endives. The roots can be added to soups and made into tea. The flowers can be added to salads, made into wine, or breaded and fried. The plant is high in potassium, calcium, vitamins A and C, and other nutrients. Dandelions have also been recognized as a medicinal herb in both Western herbal traditions and traditional Chinese medicine. They help tone internal organs, especially the liver and kidneys. Because of this, dandelions also have a strong resonance with healing. But the dandelion's ability to take so much abuse, be strong, and bounce back is an energetic model of resilience.

As we align ourselves with resilience, we can also be aware of the resilience in those around us. Plants, animals, and the earth itself exhibit resilience.

Morning Attunement Questions

- What connections do I have with dandelions and resilience?
- Where else in the green world or in my life do I observe resilience?
- What does this correspondence feel like?
- How can I describe resilience in words or pictures?
- Where does resilience resonate most strongly in or around my body or in my life?

Daily Integration Questions

- In what ways is the world reflecting dandelions or resilience back to me?
- What nuances and shades of meaning do I notice about dandelions and resilience?

Evening Reflection Questions

- Where and how did I experience dandelions or resilience today?
- How did I embrace resilience today?
- What wisdom does the dandelion's correspondence of resilience bring to my life?

Week 2
Apple and Imagination
Malus domestica

Cutting an apple in half horizontally reveals a seed chamber in the shape of a five-pointed star, the symbol of many earth-based spiritual traditions. The five points represent the elements (earth, air, fire, water) and our place in the universe (spirit). Finding meaningful patterns in the shape of a seed chamber—or anywhere in the world—is an act of imagination. Apples have a strong correspondence with imagination.

Apples are often pictured as the forbidden fruit that Eve tasted in the Garden of Eden. The traditional story doesn't end well for Eve and her companion. However, if we look at the story from Eve's point of view, she imagined herself with knowledge and wisdom and took a calculated risk.

There are thousands of apple varieties with seemingly endless differences in taste and size. It's fun to think that apples imagined themselves into these endless varieties. Apple trees do play a part, but it is more of a co-imagining with humans. Apple growers select the taste and other attributes they want in the fruit. Apple seeds embrace a kind of renegade imagination; the seeds don't usually result in the same variation of apple they came from, and these seedlings are one way that growers discover new varieties.

My dad lovingly tended apple trees throughout my childhood, so apples have a special resonance for me. Each year we'd watch the transformation from bud to flower to tiny apple and then to fruit. From the time the buds appeared, I could envision eating fresh apples, apple pie, apple upside-down cake, and apple fritters even though harvest was months away.

Imagination is creating something in our minds that does not yet exist. Imagination always precedes form, even in the simplest of actions. When we harvest garden vegetables to create dinner or pick flowers to arrange a bouquet, we are imagining the final product. From our gardens to our neighborhoods to our world, everything exists first in imagination.

The world we live in was once part of ours or someone's imagination. Stop and contemplate that for a moment. Imagination is what lets us ride the wave of moments into the future. It fuels problem-solving and creativity. Imagination allows us to picture hopeful futures and work to make positive changes in our world.

Morning Attunement Questions

- What connections do I have with apples and imagination?
- Where else in the green world or in my life do I observe imagination?
- What does this correspondence feel like?
- How can I describe the energetic attribute of imagination in words or pictures?
- Where does imagination resonate most strongly in or around my body or in my life?

Daily Integration Questions

- In what ways is the world reflecting apples or imagination back to me?
- What nuances and shades of meaning do I notice about apples and imagination?

Evening Reflection Questions

- Where and how did I experience apples or imagination today?
- How did I embrace imagination today?
- What wisdom does the apple's correspondence of imagination bring to my life?

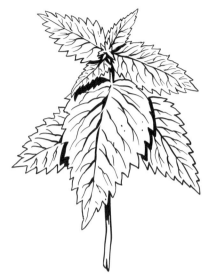

Week 3
Stinging Nettles and Prickly Gifts
Urtica dioica

If you have accidentally encountered stinging nettles while walking near a creek, the concept of a gift may not have been at the forefront of your mind. And it is easy to bump into nettles; the plant is not showy. The flowers are the same color as the plant. They fall from the leaves in an almost-invisible cascade.

Stinging nettle leaves and stems are covered with tiny hairs that deliver a potent sting when you brush against them. One of the chemicals in the stinging nettle is formic acid, a chemical that is also present in a bee sting.

If a painful sting has been your only experience with nettles, you might wonder why a plant like that even exists. But nettles have been a boon to humans. They have been used for food and medicine for thousands of years. Once cooked, the leaves no longer sting. The plant is high in iron, phosphorus, potassium, and B vitamins. Herbalists have relied on nettle tea and tinctures to support kidney function, iron deficiency, and overall health. Nettles are also fibrous and have been used for fabric since the Bronze Age.

Nettles have provided much to humans, yet their sting presents a challenge. They remind us that the world is a complicated place. Things are not simply good or bad, even though the human brain loves to categorize things in this way. The world is more complex. Challenging situations and difficult people are not wholly good or evil. When we breathe in the gifts and reframe the challenges, we might see that the world is more nuanced than black and white. It seems trite to say that difficult situations make us stronger, but in many cases they do.

If you examine some of the past difficulties in your life, you might conclude that they also brought you gifts in some way. They may have contributed to your personal growth, understanding of the world, or wisdom. When you encounter a new prickly situation, whether internal or external, consciously tune in to nettle energy and be aware of gifts and hidden value.

Morning Attunement Questions

- What connections do I have with stinging nettles and prickly gifts?
- Where else in the green world or in my life do I observe prickly gifts?
- What does this correspondence feel like?
- How can I describe the energetic attribute of prickly gifts in words or pictures?
- Where does the concept of prickly gifts resonate most strongly in or around my body or in my life?

Daily Integration Questions

- In what ways is the world reflecting stinging nettles or prickly gifts back to me?
- What nuances and shades of meaning do I notice about stinging nettles and prickly gifts?

Evening Reflection Questions

- Where and how did I experience stinging nettles or prickly gifts today?
- How did I embrace the concept of prickly gifts today?
- What wisdom does the stinging nettle's correspondence of prickly gifts bring to my life?

Rhubarb and Duality

Rheum rhabarbarum

Rhubarb is an impressive plant, a perennial vegetable with giant elephant-ear leaves and equally giant flower stalks. Rhubarb leaf stalks are edible and tart. They are often made into pies and jam with added sweetener. The leaf stalks are edible, but the leaves themselves are considered toxic. I first learned this as a child, and as a young gardener, I was fascinated by the dual nature of this plant.

Many plants have inedible parts that are too stringy or tough to eat. But rhubarb leaves are reported to have large amounts of oxalic acid, a naturally occurring substance in plants that can make one sick or even cause death if eaten in large quantities.

From that perspective, rhubarb has always had a correspondence to duality. It is one plant with healthy and toxic parts. Duality reminds us that there is unity in opposites. One cannot exist without the other.

The yin-yang symbol illustrates unity in duality. The circle is divided into two parts that curve in on themselves. One part is white. The other is black. Within each is a tiny dot of the other, reminding us that the seeds of the opposite are present. Even though the two colors appear disconnected, they are part of one whole. If we push away one part, we push away both.

Rhubarb's correspondence with duality is also about the relationship between myth and fact. Facts and myths appear as opposites, yet they are often intertwined, and each has seeds of the other. The facts that were presented to me as a new gardener were not entirely true; rhubarb leaves do contain oxalic acid, but so do the rhubarb stalks that we make into pies. Other plants that are eaten on a regular basis, like kale, beets, and spinach, also contain oxalic acid. Most people will not eat enough of these plants for oxalic acid to affect them. However, there are some individuals who are sensitive to oxalic acid and should avoid foods that contain it. Thus, there is a kernel of truth in the myth. It's based on the experience of sensitive individuals. Duality is about seeing the unity even in seemingly contradictory parts. There is an interdependence that makes up the whole.

Morning Attunement Questions

- What connections do I have with rhubarb and duality?
- Where else in the green world or in my life do I observe duality?
- What does this correspondence feel like?
- How can I describe the energetic attribute of duality in words or pictures?
- Where does the attribute of duality resonate most strongly in or around my body or in my life?

Daily Integration Questions

- In what ways is the world reflecting rhubarb or duality back to me?
- What nuances and shades of meaning do I notice with rhubarb and duality?

Evening Reflection Questions

- Where and how did I experience rhubarb or duality today?
- How did I embrace duality today?
- What wisdom does rhubarb's correspondence of duality bring to my life?

Week 5
Marigold and Optimism
Tagetes erecta

Marigolds are the common folk of the garden world. (They should not be confused with the calendula, which is called pot marigold in some parts of the world.) They are everywhere. Depending on the variety, they can resemble zinnias, daisies, or chrysanthemums. Marigolds have a unique fragrance that puts some people off, but there is a lot to love about them. They grow easily, come in a multitude of brilliant colors, reseed themselves without a lot of work on the gardener's part, and are great companion plants in an organic garden. They repel cabbage moths and are toxic to some varieties of nematodes (organisms that feed on the roots of plants). The small varieties can easily be tucked into corners of a vegetable garden, adding unexpected color, protection, and perkiness.

The seedpods are a tiny bell shape. The seeds resemble small, thin pencils. When marigold flowers are dry, the seeds slide right out, making seed collecting a great activity for young gardeners. Marigolds were some of the first flowers I was aware of as a child; my mother planted them in profusion, and I loved helping collect the seeds in the fall.

If you are not already a gardener, marigolds are a good place to start. They are one of the easiest plants in the world. Marigolds are annuals, so they put all their energy into a vivid display for one season. They flower profusely and although they prefer heat, they seem to deal well with a wide range of climates.

Marigolds vibrate with optimism. Optimism is the belief that we can get through difficulties with an expectation of positive things in the future. Marigold flowers are colorful, cheerful, and uplifting, and they have an abundance of blooms. Their ease in growing and their ability to replant themselves are both symbols of optimism; we know their beauty will return at a future date. Their presence in the garden supports other plants in a multitude of ways.

Optimism is an attribute that can be cultivated and nurtured. Sometimes the world can appear very dark, but when you look carefully, you can see it is intricately composed of both hope and darkness, difficulty and opportunity. When practicing optimism, we don't ignore the difficulties, but choose to pay attention to the positives as well. It takes a conscious retraining of your attention to focus on an expectation of positive things. And since most of us do not know what the future holds, it is a healthier practice to hold the energy of optimism. As you plant this seed for yourself, be attuned to wherever you can discover optimism around you—in people, plants, and the world.

Morning Attunement Questions

- What connections do I have with marigolds and optimism?
- Where else in the green world and my life do I observe optimism?
- What does this correspondence feel like?
- How can I describe the energetic attribute of optimism in words or pictures?
- Where does this correspondence of optimism resonate most strongly in or around my body or in my life?

Daily Integration Questions

- In what ways is the world reflecting marigolds or optimism back to me?
- What nuances and shades of meaning do I notice about marigolds and optimism?

Evening Reflection Questions

• Where and how did I experience marigolds or optimism today?

• How did I embrace optimism today?

• What wisdom does the marigold's correspondence of optimism bring to my life?

Week 6
Purple Coneflower and Boundaries
Echinacea purpurea

Purple coneflower is indigenous to North America. Long before Europeans arrived, Native Americans, especially those in the heartland of the country, had a history of using the plant to treat wounds, sore throats, infections, snake bites, and more.[15] European herbalists quickly adopted the herb because of its antimicrobial properties that reduce or eliminate bacterial, viral, and fungal infections.

Purple coneflower is also a beautiful perennial plant found in many gardens. It is hardy and dependable, and it flowers over a long period of time. The flowers are lavender or deep purple and resemble a daisy, except a center cone rises up from the flower petals. When my grandchildren were small, they learned quickly that this plant is not one that you run your hands across. It does not sting, but the cone is rough and scratchy. The word *Echinacea* comes from the Greek word *ekhinos*, which means hedgehog, a good description of the bristly cone.

The correspondence for purple coneflower is boundaries. The flower resonates with boundaries on a physical level with its rough cone that creates a tough border at the top of the plant. It also emulates boundaries on a cellular level. As a medicinal herb, it has been used to help cells create boundaries that protect them from pathogens and other invaders.

---

15. Bergner, *Healing Power of Echinacea and Goldenseal*, 13–17.

When we bring our attention to boundaries, we notice that the world is full of natural boundaries. Some are permanent, while others are more flexible. In the green world, there are hard boundaries like cliffs and river banks, but also softer boundaries when plants establish territory for themselves as their roots spread out. In our human world, we can observe hard and soft boundaries as well. Setting healthy boundaries for plants and people is an act of self-care. Healthy boundaries create some separation, but they can also be permeable. A healthy cell wall is a boundary that lets in nutrients but blocks attackers. You can energetically emulate your cell walls by doing the same in your day-to-day interactions.

When you are paying attention, you can tap into the energetic feel of boundaries. You know when someone has invaded your space or when you have softened your boundaries to allow loved ones entry. When focusing on boundaries, consider the boundaries between yourself and others or the boundaries between yourself and the green world. You might become aware of boundaries where you didn't notice them before.

Morning Attunement Questions

- What connections do I have with purple coneflowers and boundaries?

- Where else in the green world or in my life do I observe boundaries?

- What does this correspondence feel like?

- How can I describe the energetic attribute of boundaries in words or pictures?

- Where does this correspondence of boundaries resonate most strongly in or around my body or in my life?

Daily Integration Questions

- In what ways is the world reflecting purple coneflowers or boundaries back to me?

- What nuances and shades of meaning do I notice about purple coneflowers and boundaries?

Evening Reflection Questions

- Where and how did I experience purple coneflowers or boundaries today?

- How did I embrace the concept of boundaries today?

- What wisdom does the purple coneflower's correspondence of boundaries bring to my life?

Week 7
Motherwort and Courage
Leonurus cardiaca

Motherwort is a healing herb that is easy to walk by without noticing. It is part of the mint family, but it's better behaved then some of the mints. There are no flashy flowers or super strong fragrances. The serrated leaves slope downward, away from the long stem. Tiny prickly, purplish flowers develop where the leaves and stem connect. As summer progresses, the flowers morph into hard, scratchy seedpods. Motherwort reminds me of a dancer with its tall stem and leaves that resemble a ballerina's skirt. It looks delicate, but if you touch it, the tough flowers and seeds will let you know there is more to it than meets the eye.

The common name, motherwort, indicates its use by herbalists as a nourishing herb for women and female reproductive organs. *Cardiaca*, from the Latin for heart, is part of the botanical name and indicates its association with heart healing. Motherwort was a history of strengthening and gladdening the heart.[16]

The convergence of these healing properties creates motherwort's energetic correspondence of courage. Motherhood and parenting require courage at every turn to nurture and guide children in a difficult world. Having a strong heart is physically and allegorically aligned with courage. The first part of the botanical name, *Leonurus*, contains *leo*, the Latin word for lion. Some herbalists thought

---

16. Grieve, *A Modern Herbal*, vol. I, 555.

the plant resembled a lion's tail. Personally, I don't see the resemblance, but I do see this plant as lion-hearted—another way to envision courage.

Contrary to popular belief, courage is not fearlessness. Often when we embody courage, we are fully aware of potential danger and walk into the storm anyway. Courage is stepping up and doing hard things because we know we must. With courage, there is a willingness to put ourselves out in the world even though we might be rejected, ignored, or even harmed.

We sometimes frame courage as a dramatic act, like running into a burning building to rescue a child. The inconspicuous nature of motherwort reminds us that small acts of courage happen daily. When you bring your mindful attention to this plant and correspondence, you can be attentive to those small acts of courage in yourself and others.

Morning Attunement Questions

- What connections do I have with motherwort and courage?
- Where else in the green world or in my life do I observe courage?
- What does this correspondence feel like?
- How can I describe this energetic attribute of courage in words or pictures?
- Where does this correspondence of courage resonate most strongly in or around my body or in my life?

Daily Integration Questions

- In what ways is the world reflecting motherwort or courage back to me?
- What nuances and shades of meaning do I notice about motherwort and courage?

Evening Reflection Questions

- Where and how did I experience motherwort or courage today?
- How did I embrace courage today?
- What wisdom does motherwort's correspondence of courage bring to my life?

Week 8
Amaranth and Grace
Amaranthus cruentus

Amaranth is an ancient plant, sacred to the Aztecs. When the Spanish invaders arrived, they tried to eradicate the plant because it was intertwined with Aztec spiritual practices. Thankfully, the Spanish invaders were unsuccessful.[17]

The correspondence for amaranth is grace, and it has a dual meaning. The physical form of the plant radiates elegance and grace. It is a tall plant that can grow up to eight feet tall. In the summer, long plumes in shades of scarlet and orange sway gently in the wind. In the fall, if the seeds are left unharvested, thousands of them shake loose from the plant, cascading to the ground over a period of weeks like tiny rainstorms.

The word grace also has the connotation of a kind of cosmic gift or blessing. It's not a blessing achieved by effort, just a gift freely given by the infinite. A state of grace feels like a portal opens and blessings flow through from the universe. Amaranth was sacred to the Aztecs for many reasons, not the least of which is it sustained them and was perceived as a gift from the gods.

Amaranth is a tough plant; it can be grown in places where it is difficult to grow other plants. It thrives in hot weather and is drought resistant. It is also incredibly nutritious—the seeds are high in protein and can be made into flour. In addition to protein, amaranth contains other important nutrients like

17. Cole, *Amaranth*, 17.

magnesium, phosphorus, and iron. The leaves are also edible as salad greens or when cooked.

A plant that sustained the Aztecs in a harsh environment was indeed a cosmic gift, and it created a state of grace. Attuning yourself to grace allows you to shift your awareness to the ways you are supported every day by the earth itself, by other species, and by your community. Like the Aztecs, you could focus daily on the flow of blessings that keeps you alive. Perhaps all life on the planet is an act of grace.

Morning Attunement Questions

- What connections do I have with amaranth and grace?
- Where else in the green world or in my life do I observe grace?
- What does this correspondence feel like?
- How can I describe grace in words or pictures?
- Where does this correspondence of grace resonate most strongly in or around my body or in my life?

Daily Integration Questions

- In what ways is the world reflecting amaranth or grace back to me?
- What nuances and shades of meaning do I notice about amaranth and grace?

Evening Reflection Questions

- Where and how did I experience amaranth or grace today?
- How did I embrace the energy of grace today?
- What wisdom does amaranth's correspondence of grace bring to my life?

Week 9
Borage and Wildness
Borago officinalis

Borage is an unwieldy plant that can grow up to two feet tall. The edible flow-ers are a vibrant blue and shaped like five-pointed stars. The flowers taste like cucumber and look beautiful in summer salads, and the leaves can be used for a refreshing tea. It is also fun to make ice cubes with borage flowers frozen inside for summer drinks. Herbalists have recommended borage for depression and the treatment of fevers. Borage is a great companion plant because it attracts bees and repels some insect pests. The only danger is that borage can crowd out other plants; it is an annual that reseeds easily, so you may have to pull out some of the extras that spring up each year.

With its sprawling branches and leaves covered with scratchy hairs, borage feels a bit wild, which is the correspondence for this plant. For people who prefer a carefully ordered and manicured garden, borage may not be the best fit.

It might surprise some gardeners that some gardening methods (like per-maculture and biodynamics) recommend leaving a wild, untended area in your garden. It can provide a habitat for helpful insects and other critters. It's also a way to let the soil rest and to observe what plants grow naturally in your soil. In the famous Findhorn garden, a wild space was set aside for the plant spirits to reside.[18]

---

18. The Findhorn Community, *Findhorn Garden*, 25.

Your comfort level with wildness—in your garden and in your life—may be in how you define the word wild. Borage feels wild because it is a little disordered, but there is beauty with the wildness. Wildness could also be defined as something edgy or even dangerous, and that definition has negative connotations.

If you carefully observe the places that are ordered in the world, you may notice disarray and wildness doing their best to pop up: wild plants break through cracks in pavement; vines creep up the walls of buildings; wildflowers quickly establish themselves in empty lots. Order may be something humans attempt to impress on the world, and wild disorder may be the state it wants to return to.

As you mindfully work with this word and plant, be aware of the places in and around your life that have a wild nature. Notice where the wild is emerging, in your green space and in your life. You might want to contemplate if you need more or less wildness in your life.

Morning Attunement Questions

- What connections do I have with borage or wildness?
- Where else in the green world do I observe wildness?
- What does this correspondence feel like?
- How can I describe this energetic attribute of wildness in words or pictures?
- Where does this correspondence of wildness resonate most strongly in or around my body or in my life?

Daily Integration Questions

- In what ways is the world reflecting borage and wildness back to me?
- What nuances and shades of meaning do I notice about borage or wildness?
- Does wildness feel fun and interesting or tense and out of control?

Evening Reflection Questions

- Where and how did I experience borage or wildness today?
- How did I embrace wildness today?
- What wisdom does borage's correspondence of wildness bring to my life?

Week 10
Clover and Nurturing
Trifolium spp.

Growing up, the other neighborhood children and I often hunted for four-leaf clovers. I don't remember any of us ever finding one, although sometimes friends tried to fake a four-leaf clover by twisting a fourth leaf around the usual three. There are many varieties of clover; most people are familiar with white clover, which is common in lawns. The small whitish globe is a favorite of bees and other pollinators. Red clover, which is taller and has a larger flower head, has been used as a healing herb for respiratory concerns, skin conditions, and its general restorative qualities. All clover leaves and flowers are edible, and the red clover looks beautiful in salads. Clover flowers can be brewed for a sweet-tasting tea with a mild anise flavor.

Clover is in the family of plants known as the nitrogen fixers. Nitrogen fixing is an important function in the green world because nitrogen is essential for plant growth, but it is not always available to plants. The element is plentiful in the air; however, most plants can't access it that way. Clover and other legumes have a relationship with nitrogen-collecting soil bacteria. The bacteria live in nodules on the roots of clover, pulling nitrogen from the air and converting it to an accessible form. When clover dies or is cut back, the nitrogen is released and made available to the soil and surrounding plants.

Clover provides this vital function for other plants and defines its energetic correspondence of nurturing. Nurturing provides or creates an environment where living organisms can be their best selves, one where they can blossom and come to fruition.

Nurturing is not always visible. If you dig up a clover plant, you could observe the nodules on the roots where bacteria are collecting nitrogen, but you wouldn't be able to see what is happening. If you consider the nurturing role of parents, much of it is out of sight or incomprehensible to small children. It's hard to explain to a child that going off to work and paying the mortgage is a way of nurturing them. There are hundreds of things parents do to provide a nurturing environment for their children, but they are not always visible.

Of course, nurturing is not something that only belongs to parents. Any time energy is focused on creating healthy environments, nurturing is taking place. It happens in communities, neighborhoods, and families, and it's often part of the background unless you intentionally look for it. Planting trees and creating green space is a way to nurture communities. Family meals and quality time are a way to nurture your family and friends. Being intentional about self-care is a way to nurture yourself.

While holding on to this correspondence for the week, first be aware of how the green world nurtures and supports us by making life possible. Then observe where nurturing is happening in your life, relationships, and neighborhood.

Sometimes the lack of nurturing is what is most visible. In considering this correspondence, you can shift that perspective and tune in to the nurturing that is happening in the background, often unnoticed. Notice what is nurturing you and how you nurture others.

Morning Attunement Questions

- What connections do I have with clover and nurturing?
- Where else in the green world or in my life do I observe nurturing?
- What does this correspondence feel like?
- How can I describe the energetic attribute of nurturing in words or pictures?
- Where does this correspondence of nurturing resonate most strongly in or around my body or in my life?

Daily Integration Questions

- In what ways is the world reflecting clover and nurturing back to me?
- What nuances and shades of meaning do I notice about clover and nurturing?

Evening Reflection Questions

- Where and how did I experience clover or nurturing today?
- How did I embrace nurturing today?
- What wisdom does clover's correspondence of nurturing bring to my life?

Week 11

Garlic and Confidence

Allium sativum

My general rule for garlic in recipes is to double it; two cloves really means four, and three means six. In the Italian American household of my childhood, my mom used garlic liberally in the kitchen. My father grew pounds of garlic each year; we have pictures of my children and their cousins holding braided strings. Garlic was a kitchen staple, like having salt and pepper.

I remember being in my early twenties and discovering that not everyone thought of garlic this way. I was helping a friend make dinner, a basic stir-fry, and asked where she kept the garlic. She looked confused, then said she didn't keep garlic anywhere. That seemed completely unthinkable to me.

Garlic graces my garden as well as my kitchen. Garlic cloves, the smallest section of a garlic bulb, are planted in the fall and begin to grow underground before winter. They wait out the winter without showing themselves and then, when spring arrives, they are ready to send out green shoots. Garlic is a member of the lily family, and the mature stems stand tall with slender leaves. By mid-summer, the plant creates a full garlic bulb ready for harvest.

Garlic has a long history as a healing plant across many cultures. As it is anti-microbial, garlic can play a part in reducing infections, whether viral or bacterial. It was used as an antiseptic on wounds during World War I.[19] It supports overall bronchial health and heart health.

The energetic correspondence for garlic is confidence—a very exuberant confidence. Garlic announces itself clearly. Whether in a prepared dish or while chopping it in the kitchen, it is apparent that garlic is in the house. With its fiery flavor and zest, it doesn't do things halfway.

Confidence is about knowing who and what you are and presenting that face to the world. Garlic is a great energetic role model. Confidence eliminates self-doubt. You cultivate an awareness of your own worth and know what you stand for, whether others agree or not. When you are confident, you let your own unique flavor shine.

As you focus on confidence this week, pay attention to your own confidence and what causes it to ebb and flow. Note the confidence of others and how it affects their lives and those around them.

Morning Attunement Questions
- What connections do I have with garlic and confidence?
- Where else in the green world or in my life do I observe confidence?
- What does this correspondence feel like?
- How can I describe confidence in words or pictures?
- Where does this correspondence of confidence resonate most strongly in or around my body or in my life?

Daily Integration Questions
- In what ways is the world reflecting garlic or confidence back to me?
- What nuances and shades of meaning do I notice about garlic and confidence?

Evening Reflection Questions
- Where and how did I experience garlic or confidence today?
- How did I embrace confidence today?
- What wisdom does garlic's correspondence of confidence bring to my life?

---

19. Bergner, *Healing Power of Garlic*, 23.

Week 12

Rose and Tradition

Rosa spp.

My grandmother and mother both loved roses and had small, traditional-looking rose gardens. Individual roses were tidily pruned and beautifully displayed. They were solitary plants, without the interplanting of any other flowers. I found this curious as a child because this orderly rose garden contrasted with my mother's annual beds, which were a riot of different plants and colors. While I could appreciate the beauty of individual roses, I was a much bigger fan of the wild beds. The rose beds seemed formal and rigid.

In the story of *Alice in Wonderland*, there is a scene where a perplexed Alice discovers the gardeners painting the roses red.[20] The gardeners are terrified the queen will find out they've planted the wrong color roses. It is a commentary on the whims of the monarchy, but as a child it aligned with my thoughts that roses have something to do with order and rules of correctness.

I've come to appreciate roses as an adult, and I've also realized that some roses can be quite brambly and wild—it's humans who do the pruning and make decisions about how to display them.

The rose's energetic correspondence is tradition. As some of the first cultivated flowers, they have been used for medicine, food, perfume, and beauty.

---

20. Carroll, *The Annotated Alice*, 96.

There are hundreds of varieties in a multitude of colors, so it's no surprise that roses are intertwined with human culture and tradition. It's enlightening to see how those traditions and associations have changed over time. Ancient Egyptians embraced roses as symbols of love and beauty, similar to current society. During the early Roman era, they were a symbol of secrets and confidentiality. Roses became a sign of celebration and revelry during the Roman Empire. Rose petals were scattered before triumphant armies and strewn at feasts and weddings. Over time, the revelry escalated and roses became associated with decadence. Then, as Christianity took over in Europe, the rose changed to a symbol of purity, often being associated with Mary, the mother of Jesus. Roses were also used as symbols of the distinct clans involved in the fifteenth-century Wars of the Roses; one family adopted the white rose and the other chose red.[21]

In *Seven Flowers and How They Shaped the World*, Jennifer Potter notes, "The real power of the rose lies in the way people from different societies and different ages have used the flower to say something about themselves, in effect transforming the rose into a symbol of deeply held values—cultural, religious, political—or simply using the rose to tell their stories."[22]

Tradition is about maintaining the existing order. It prescribes a certain way of doing and being. The customs and rituals created by tradition provide structure and a feeling of safety. Tradition helps people belong—that's the beautiful part. However, tradition can result in bias and judgment for anyone who doesn't embrace said tradition. There may be a rigid belief system and rules that are difficult to change. Both aspects of tradition are real; it's not an either-or.

When focusing on the correspondence of the rose, be attentive to your familial and cultural traditions. Stepping back to notice and appreciate them, also be aware of needed changes. Mindfulness with this correspondence involves exploring methods to root yourself in tradition as you branch out to explore other ways of being in the world. Consider the energy of tradition and where on the spectrum—from safety to rigidity—your personal orientation with tradition lies.

---

21. Potter, *Seven Flowers*, 133–62.
22. Potter, *Seven Flowers*, 146.

Morning Attunement Questions

- What connections do I have with roses and tradition?
- Where else in the green world or in my life do I observe traditions?
- What does this correspondence feel like?
- How can I describe the energetic attribute of tradition in words or pictures?
- Where does this correspondence of tradition resonate most strongly in or around my body or in my life?

Daily Integration Questions

- In what ways is the world reflecting roses or tradition back to me?
- What nuances and shades of meaning do I notice about roses or tradition?

Evening Reflection Questions

- Where and how did I experience roses or tradition today?
- How did I embrace tradition today?
- What wisdom does the rose's correspondence of tradition bring to my life?

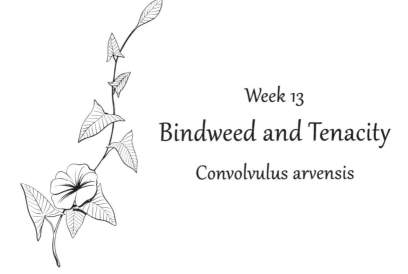

Week 13
Bindweed and Tenacity
Convolvulus arvensis

Bindweed, at first glance, seems like a lovely plant. Delicate white and pink flowers emerge across the length of a trailing vine; it resembles the morning glory plant. Bindweed lives up to its name by growing quickly, wrapping and binding itself around anything in its vicinity.

Aboveground, the growth seems exponential, and keeping up with it is almost impossible. If you dig up bindweed, you'll see that the roots mirror the curving spiral action of the aboveground plant. They spread and weave themselves through the soil. When you try to extract the roots, some parts inevitably break off and start new plants. The flowers also form little seed heads that release hundreds of seeds, so the plant can spread in multiple ways.

I've tried all the usual organic methods to get rid of bindweed without much lasting success. These have included covering it with cardboard and then mulch, digging it up, and pouring vinegar and dish soap on it. Part of the problem is that my neighborhood is awash in bindweed, and this tenacious plant is winning in the yards that border mine. Bindweed embodies the the trait of holding on tightly.

I might not like bindweed, but I can appreciate this trait of tenacity. Stubbornly holding on can be a good or bad thing, depending on the situation. Being tenacious about a personal goal or plan—hanging on tightly and giving it all your energy and focus—will help you succeed. On the other hand, if you stubbornly hang on to ideas, people, or things that you'd be better off releasing, this could be a problem. Tenacity can also be a challenge if you have situations or people in your life that have wrapped themselves around you in a bindweed-like fashion. You may need to step back and make a plan to extricate yourself.

The energy of tenacity has both strengths and challenges. Meet the challenges with your own tenacity by hanging on to healthy and positive choices for yourself. Pay mindful attention to where you see tenacity popping up in yourself or others.

Morning Attunement Questions

- What connections do I have with bindweed and tenacity?
- Where else in the green world or in my life do I observe tenacity?
- What does this correspondence feel like?
- How can I describe this energetic attribute of tenacity in words or pictures?
- Where does this correspondence of tenacity resonate most strongly in or around my body or in my life?

Daily Integration Questions

- In what ways is the world reflecting bindweed or tenacity back to me?
- What nuances and shades of meaning do I notice about bindweed and tenacity?

Evening Reflection Questions

- Where and how did I experience bindweed or tenacity today?
- How did I embrace the energy of tenacity today?
- What wisdom does bindweed's correspondence of tenacity bring to my life?

Week 14

Crocus and Hope

Crocus spp.

For those of us who live through winter each year, signs of spring are happy events. Crocuses, the tiny cup-shaped flowers that appear as winter is waning, are messengers of better days ahead. The flowers come in a range of happy, bright colors. Pushing up from the ground, often through a blanket of snow, they seem to say, "Enough already!"

Crocuses are perennials and will continue to create new plants and grow each year. They can be sown right in the lawn because the flowers will be gone before it is time to mow. With just a little effort to get them in the ground, your yard can have an ongoing sign of spring hopefulness.

The energetic correspondence for crocuses is hope. They pop up at just the right time to remind us that spring will eventually arrive. Denver, Colorado, where I live, can have snow on the ground in May—hopeful reminders are necessary! Crocuses are well-suited to carry the energy of hope in the garden. The leaves have a waxy coating that allows them to withstand the snow. They also stay low to the ground, so bitter winds are less likely to take them out.

In the wellness workshops I facilitate, we often talk about the importance of hope. It's a vital component to health and well-being. Being hopeful strengthens our immune system and helps us find our way through difficult situations. However, hope can feel elusive. It can be challenging to find hope if we don't

have it. Some of us are wired to be more hopeful, but we can all learn to cultivate hope in a more intentional way.

In most cases, crocuses do not appear on their own. Someone planted them.
Just like crocuses, human hopefulness may need some thought and planning.
We can approach hope in that way, finding intentional ways to plant seeds of
hope for ourselves and others.

One regular practice for me is to check in with websites and podcasts that
inform me about the positive work happening on the planet. They don't sugar-
coat things. It's not about pretending there aren't challenges, but rather tuning
in to the way people are coming together to meet challenges.

Crocuses emerge in the world with a protective coating and hunker down
low to the ground. Think about how to apply those concepts in your own
attempts to hold on to hope. Hunkering down can be about knowing your circle
of influence and staying focused on that, rather than thinking about the entire
world. You can also nurture your protective coating by taking care of yourself by
getting enough sleep and reducing stress, for example. Those small steps alone
can change your view of the world and lift your feelings of hopefulness.

As you turn a mindful focus toward hope, examine how others hold hope.
Learn and draw inspiration from their examples. For example, I regularly read
biographies of people who have made it through difficult situations; understanding how they stayed hopeful and motivated provides me with concepts I
can use in my own life.

Morning Attunement Questions

- What connections do I have with crocuses and hope?

- Where else in the green world or in my life do I observe hope?

- What does this correspondence feel like?

- How can I describe this energetic attribute of hope in words or
  pictures?

- Where does this correspondence of hope resonate most strongly in or
  around my body or in my life?

Daily Integration Questions

- In what ways is the world reflecting crocuses or hope back to me?
- What nuances and shades of meaning do I notice about crocuses and hope?

Evening Reflection Questions

- Where and how did I experience crocuses or hope today?
- How did I embrace hope today?
- What insights do I have about crocuses or hope?
- What wisdom does the crocus's correspondence of hope bring to my life?

Week 15
Rue and Warding Off
Ruta graveolens

The bluish-green color of rue may catch your attention in a summer garden, but it is not a showy plant. The small yellow flowers that appear in midsummer are easily overshadowed by flashier herbs and perennials. However, in a winter garden, rue becomes a star attraction, as it keeps its distinctive leaves throughout the cold months. It is a beautiful reminder that there is life out in the snow.

The name rue comes from the Greek word meaning "to set free." It was thought to free people from illness, insects, evil, and even venomous snake bites. Judges in the Middle Ages kept rue in their courtroom to ward off fleas and diseases.[23]

Rue is one of the plants often used in Four Thieves Vinegar, a vinegar-based tincture that prevents infection and illness. This mixture has a dark history, as it was reputedly used by thieves robbing the homes of the dead during the plague.

In *A Modern Herbal*, Maude Grieve tells us, "Rue has been regarded from the earliest times as successful in warding off contagion."[24] Warding off is rue's energetic correspondence. It invokes images of both protection and pushing away. This idea aligns nicely with the tai chi move called "ward off." This is a protective action in which the arm comes up to block as the leg steps out

---

23. Grieve, *A Modern Herbal*, vol. II, 695.
24. Ibid.

at an angle. Like most movements in tai chi, there are elements of using balance and body position to repel an attacker. This movement is not about meeting force with a lot of force or, alternatively, hunkering down in a defensive stance. When done correctly, it is about using structure and intention to deflect incoming negative energy. Unlike boundaries, which create a wall to stop an incoming power, the ward off move seeks to deflect and redirect the negative, all with minimal effort on our part. It is a neutralizing and turning away of energy, rather than crashing into the incoming strength. When executed well, it can appear subtle and effortless.

While mindfully considering rue and its correspondence, pay attention to where in your life the concept of warding off might be of value. Remember that it is about structure and deflection, not about a great use of energy or force. Consider how to create that energetic structure for yourself on a regular basis. As you observe those around you, you may notice others successfully putting this concept to work.

Morning Attunement Questions

- What connections do I have with rue and the concept of warding off?
- Where else in the green world or in my life do I observe the concept of warding off?
- What does this correspondence feel like?
- How can I describe this energetic attribute of warding off in words or pictures?
- Where does this correspondence of warding off resonate most strongly in or around my body or in my life?

Daily Integration Questions

- In what ways is the world reflecting rue or the concept of warding off back to me?
- What nuances and shades of meaning do I notice about rue and warding off?

Evening Reflection Questions

- Where and how did I experience rue or the concept of warding off today?

- How did I embrace today's attribute of warding off?

- What wisdom does the rue's correspondence of warding off bring to my life?

Week 16
Clary Sage and Clarity
Salvia sclarea

Clary sage, like its sister plant common sage, is strongly aromatic. The fragrance is musky and earthy, not at all flowery. Unlike common sage, clary is a biennial and only lives for two years. Its first year, clary sage produces a rosette of leaves close to the ground. In its second year, the stalk features pale lavender or white flowers with pronounced bottom lips. The flowers are enfolded by small lavender-colored leaves, so the whole stalk is alive with a range of purplish colors.

One of the many traditional uses of clary sage was as an eye wash. The seeds are mucilaginous (sticky), and soaking them in warm water for a few minutes creates a liquid that is helpful for washing debris out of the eye. Other names for the plant, like Clear Eye, See Bright, and Eyebright, reflect this use of the plant. Clary sage is most popular today for making essential oils.

Clarity, the correspondence for this plant, can almost be heard in clary sage's name. Clarity is a state of transparency and clearness. It is a word often used when describing gemstones, which are rated by their cloudiness and transparency. Clary sage resonates with clear vision, which is a kind of wisdom.

In the early days of my women's ritual group, we'd meet at the full moon and declare intentions. Mine were always about clarity. I longed for a crystal-clear vision of how to proceed in life. Many moons have passed since then, and I've come to understand that perfect clarity, as one might find in a gemstone, may be impossible. Everyone has cultural, familial, and human biases that muddy our vision. The world we think we know is more complicated than it appears. We are limited by our senses and our ability to predict the actions of others.

We don't have to give up on achieving clarity, however. Rather than thinking of clarity as being able to clearly see the road in front of you, you might reframe the concept as simply knowing you are on the right road. Do this by tuning in to your values and choosing a direction based on those values. The path itself might not be clear, but you have clarity of purpose and direction. The wisdom is in knowing yourself and following your inner guidance. Clarity is an energetic feeling when you are aligned with your life purpose and proceed in the right direction, without knowing the outcome.

Immersing yourself in the green world can help you find clarity. Being in a garden can provide a respite from overthinking and help you clear your minds. There may be places in the garden that provide a feeling of clearness, openness, and clarity. Take advantage of that energy when seeking clarity about an issue or concern.

Morning Attunement Questions

- What connections do I have with clary sage and clarity?
- Where else in the green world or in my life do I observe clarity?
- What does this correspondence feel like?
- How can I describe this energetic attribute of clarity in words or pictures?
- Where does the correspondence of clarity resonate most strongly in or around my body or in my life?

Daily Integration Questions

- In what ways is the world reflecting clary sage or clarity back to me?
- What nuances and shades of meaning do I notice about clary sage and clarity?

Evening Reflection Questions

- Where and how did I experience clary sage or clarity today?
- How did I embrace clarity today?
- What wisdom does clary sage's correspondence of clarity bring to my life?

Week 17
Lemon Balm and Renewal
Melissa officinalis

Lemon balm is a bushy perennial that releases a delightful lemony fragrance when brushed against. It's great to plant near walkways for that reason. As a member of the mint family, it can be a little wild, so sequestering it to a large planter might be preferable to releasing it in your yard.

Leaves of lemon balm can be added to salad or made into tea. The tea has a mild lemon flavor that is not as strong as the plant's fragrance would suggest. I like to make a tea of half lemon balm and half nettles. The nettles make it more robust and nutritious, while the lemon balm improves the flavor of the nettles.

Lemon balm has historically been used to counteract melancholy and anxiety. The citrusy smell vibrates with an energy of renewal, a kind of antidote for melancholy that is also the plant's correspondence.

Renewal means starting over, sweeping out the old and beginning again. It's a metaphorical throwing open of our energetic windows. We sweep away what no longer nourishes us or what is no longer relevant in our lives. It's not an accident that many cleaning supplies have a lemony smell; the scent is clean and fresh, and renewal is a clean and fresh start. It's a deep, cleansing breath for all areas of life.

The world of energy is in constant motion. If you mindfully pay attention, you'll notice that some things are depleting, and others are renewing. There is a balance in the world, but you personally might be spending too much time with depleting energy. Certainly, our on-the-move culture is aligned with depletion. In attending to renewal, be aware of this balance of energy and consciously align yourself with renewing energy when you need it. Be aware of where this energy is manifesting—and also where it is not. Be attentive to activities, people, habits, and thoughts that renew and refresh you, as well as those that don't.

Morning Attunement Questions

- What connections do I have with lemon balm and renewal?
- Where else in the green world or in my life do I observe renewal?
- What does this correspondence feel like?
- How can I describe this energetic attribute of renewal in words or pictures?
- Where does renewal resonate most strongly in or around my body or in my life?

Daily Integration Questions

- In what ways is the world reflecting lemon balm or renewal back to me?
- What nuances and shades of meaning do I notice about lemon balm and renewal?

Evening Reflection Questions

- Where and how did I experience lemon balm or renewal today?
- How did I embrace renewal today?
- What wisdom does lemon balm's correspondence of renewal bring to my life?

Week 18

Rainbow Chard and Beauty

Beta vulgaris subsp. vulgaris

"Nana, someone painted your garden." Those were the words of wonder from my three-year-old granddaughter as she stared wide-eyed at the vegetable garden. I had no idea what she was talking about until I followed her gaze to the brilliant-colored stalks and leaves of my rainbow chard.

My yard overflows with brightly colored flowers, but seeing those colors in the vegetable garden surprised her. I know that rainbow chard is pretty—that's why I choose to plant it instead of chard's plainer varieties. However, it wasn't until my granddaughter pointed out the obvious that I stopped and fully appreciated it. It did indeed look like someone had taken acrylic paints to the garden.

Most flowers have an energetic connection to beauty, and any of them would make a fine representative for beauty. What is special about the rainbow chard's energetic correspondence to beauty is the unexpected part. It surprises us with its beauty.

Chard, a member of the beet family, is also a super food. It's nutrient dense, which means it has few calories but lots of nutrients. It provides lots of magnesium, potassium, and iron as well as vitamins C, A, and K. Eating a diet full of high-nutrient vegetables can create glowing health and beauty. Any type of chard will provide that nutritional value, but rainbow chard will light up your garden *and* your dinner plate.

Rainbow chard's correspondence with beauty includes energetic and spiritual beauty. You can acknowledge beauty in all its forms, adjusting your vision to notice more beauty in and around your life. Allow yourself to be aware of, and surprised by, beauty in unexpected places.

Morning Attunement Questions

- What connections do I have with rainbow chard and beauty, especially unexpected beauty?
- Where else in the green world or in my life do I observe unexpected beauty?
- What does this correspondence feel like?
- How can I describe this energetic attribute of beauty in words or pictures?
- Where does this correspondence of unexpected beauty resonate most strongly in or around my body or in my life?

Daily Integration Questions

- In what ways is the world reflecting rainbow chard or beauty back to me?
- What nuances and shades of meaning do I notice about rainbow chard and beauty?

Evening Reflection Questions

- Where and how did I experience rainbow chard or unexpected beauty today?
- How did I embrace beauty today?
- What wisdom does rainbow chard's correspondence of beauty bring to my life?

Week 19
Lavender and Kindness
Lavandula angustifolia

Lavender is a shrubby plant with thin and fragrant grey-green leaves. It resembles rosemary until it begins to flower. In the summer, the plant sends out long stalks covered with small purple flowers. Both the leaves and flowers are fragrant; lavender is popular in foods, herbal medicines, and perfumes. If you are making a culinary creation, just a small amount of lavender is needed, as it can be overpowering otherwise. Lavender often appears in the popular spice mix Herbs de Provence, where it is balanced out by other herbs.

I've recently started making lavender syrup by using the flowers and agave. It adds a unique taste to lemonade, coffee, and other drinks. The leaves and flowers can both be made into an herbal tea, but because of the strong flavor, it is best to blend lavender with other herbs like lemon balm. The smell of lavender is calming and restorative, which is why it is often used in bath oils and bath salts. Immersing yourself in a lavender bath is one way to be kind to yourself.

The soft leaves, sweet fragrance, and restorative nature of the plant correspond to kindness. In bringing mindful attention to lavender and its correspondence, you can adopt the practice of leading with kindness. Beginning in your home court, consider how you are kind to yourself—or not. Without judgment, pay attention to how you talk to yourself and about yourself. As you step out into the world, it is possible to use this same process without judgment to notice your interactions with others. If kindness is sometimes lacking, you may decide to embrace it in a more intentional way.

Being attentive to where kindness is manifesting in the world can bring hope. If you are aligning only to the media news, you may miss the fact that big and small acts of kindness are happening all the time—they just don't get reported on the endless news sites that favor tragedy, gossip, and innuendo. That's not to say we should put our heads in the sand about challenging things happening in our world. However, when we shift our awareness to taking in kindness, we see how it works to counterbalance the negatives.

Leading with kindness, even in difficult situations, is a good mindfulness practice for challenging times. While focusing on kindness, pay close attention to your feelings about kindness and how they shift depending on if you are giving or receiving kindness.

Morning Attunement Questions

- What connections do I have with lavender and kindness?
- Where else in the green world or in my life do I observe kindness?
- What does this correspondence feel like?
- How can I describe this energetic attribute of kindness in words or pictures?
- Where does this correspondence of kindness resonate most strongly in or around my body or in my life?

Daily Integration Questions

- In what ways is the world reflecting lavender or kindness back to me?
- What nuances and shades of meaning do I notice about lavender and kindness?

Evening Reflection Questions

- Where and how did I experience lavender or kindness today?
- How did I embrace kindness today?
- What wisdom does lavender's correspondence of kindness bring to my life?

Week 20

Bee Balm and Whimsy
Monarda didyma

Bee balm is a member of the mint family, and like many mints, the leaves and flowers are edible. The brightly colored flowers liven up salads with their sweet, citrusy taste. Tea made from the leaves has been recommended by herbalists to counter stress and anxiety. Butterflies and bees love this plant, and it is an easy-to-grow addition to a pollinator or butterfly garden. Like most mints, bee balm sends out shoots along the ground to take over nearby areas, so be aware of that when you plant it.

Bee balm resonates with whimsy, an unexpected quirkiness and playfulness. The flowers look like tufts of unkempt hair in bright red, pinks, and purples. They could easily be at home as characters in a Dr. Seuss book. Occasionally, a stem emerges from the center of one flower and another tuft blooms atop the first, creating an even more unique and comical look. Bee balm flowers always make me smile, and that seems to be the point of whimsy, if there is one at all.

We could probably use more whimsy in the world. Whimsical things are pleasant oddities that pop up in weird places. They feel silly and lighthearted. If you have a serious outlook on life, you may feel that focusing on whimsy is frivolous. However, whimsy provides relief from the challenges and serious side of life. It can shift your mood and provide a tiny respite so that you can focus on more serious things with a calmer mind. When you mindfully work with this plant energy, be alert to where whimsy is showing up in the world. You may be surprised to find more whimsy than you imagined.

Morning Attunement Questions

- What connections do I have with bee balm and whimsy?
- Where else in the green world or in my life do I observe whimsy?
- What does this correspondence feel like?
- How can I describe this energetic attribute of whimsy in words or pictures?
- Where does this correspondence of whimsy resonate most strongly in or around my body or in my life?

Daily Integration Questions

- In what ways is the world reflecting bee balm or whimsy back to me?
- What nuances and shades of meaning do I notice about bee balm and whimsy?

Evening Reflection Questions

- Where and how did I experience bee balm or whimsy today?
- How did I embrace whimsy today?
- What insights do I have about bee balm or whimsy?
- What wisdom does bee balm's correspondence of whimsy bring to my life?

Week 21

Radish and Accomplishment

Raphanus sativus

Radishes are vegetables often relegated to second-string status. They may show up on the vegetable tray or as a few slices tossed into a salad. You wouldn't know this from the usual grocery store collection, but radishes come in many beautiful colors, shapes, and sizes. Check out a seed catalog and you'll find a host of different-looking radishes with flavors ranging from mild to spicy. Radishes can be a vegetable dish in their own right; try steaming or roasting them. They can, of course, be included in other vegetable medleys as well. Eaten raw, they are a great low-calorie snack food with generous amounts of potassium, calcium, and vitamin C.

In the garden, radishes are one of the fastest-growing vegetables. They are often recommended for children's gardens, as they reward impatient young gardeners with a harvest in just a few weeks. Older gardeners appreciate this trait as well.

The correspondence for radish is accomplishment. This reflects their quick harvest turnaround. Radishes give you an early boost of success as you wait for other crops to mature. Radishes also reflect a kind of overlooked accomplishment in how they are often passed over as vegetables. Their energy is about the small accomplishments we sometimes ignore.

You may downplay the mini-steps and small achievements that move you through life. It is easy to be so focused on a long-term goal that you don't fully appreciate your small successes. While it is great to have big goals and projects, focusing on smaller, everyday accomplishments taps into the beauty of each moment.

When you tune in to life as it is unfolding, you begin to acknowledge all your efforts and accomplishments. There may be days when you feel off-balance or under the weather, but you still go to work. There may be times in a busy household where you wish for peace and quiet, but you are patient with your family. You might be tired after a long day of work but still make time to check in with a friend or family member who is sick or feeling down. Each of these choices are accomplishments.

Radish energy also applies to recognizing the efforts of those around you and acknowledging that most people are doing the best they can at any given time. Appreciate whatever steps others are taking. If you are working to improve your community in some way, radish energy helps you celebrate incremental steps that take you closer to your larger goal. It is easy to feel frustrated that your life isn't perfect; radish energy helps you acknowledge the successes already achieved.

Morning Attunement Questions

- What connections do I have with radishes and accomplishment?
- Where else in the green world or in my life do I observe accomplishment?
- What does this correspondence feel like?
- How can I describe this energetic attribute of accomplishment in words or pictures?
- Where does this correspondence of accomplishment resonate most strongly in or around my body or in my life?

Daily Integration Questions

- In what ways is the world reflecting radishes or accomplishment back to me?
- What nuances and shades of meaning do I notice about radishes and accomplishment?

Evening Reflection Questions

• Where and how did I experience radishes or accomplishment today?

• How did I embrace this attribute of accomplishment today?

• What wisdom does the radish's correspondence of accomplishment bring to my life?

Week 22
Iris and Transcendence
Iris spp.

When I was a child, one of our neighbors had a large garden bed devoted to irises that fascinated me each spring. My siblings and I would pass their yard on the way to elementary school, and I was struck by the otherworldliness of the flowers. They were unlike anything my mother planted in her flower beds and resembled the orchid corsages that women wore on Mother's Day. They were mysterious and sensual. The large, multi-colored petals were dramatically frilled, some rising up and others curving down, hiding the center of the flower. Sometimes a downward-curving petal appeared to have a fuzzy caterpillar climbing out of the plant, but it was all part of the flower.

I never considered planting irises as an adult. My focus with gardening has always been on edible plants and medicinal herbs, but I also assumed irises were hard to grow. When I moved into my Denver home a number of years ago, I inherited irises from the previous owner. I quickly discovered that they are some of the easiest flowers to maintain here in our dry climate. They now light up my yard each spring with their impressive otherworldliness.

The flowers are named after Iris, the Greek goddess of rainbows, a perfect name for the multi-colored flowers. Both rainbows and the iris flower resonate with transcendence, the correspondence for this plant. Transcendence is an awareness of something beyond three-dimensional existence. It is an experience of deeper meanings and connections.

The goddess Iris was also a messenger for the gods. Transcendent experiences are a message to wake up and notice the luminous wonder all around us. Anything that shakes us out of our ordinary perceptions can be transcendent. People often think that transcendent experiences must involve big events, like the birth of a child or visiting the Grand Canyon. However, anything that shakes us out of our routine perceptions can be transcendent. Transcendence can be precipitated by seemingly ordinary moments.

Transcendent experiences can be cultivated by focus and attention. As you practice mindfulness on a regular basis, you will realize there are no ordinary days or moments. Each moment in our short human incarnation is different and precious. While holding this correspondence in your awareness, meet each moment with curiosity and the expectation that transcendence will arise.

Morning Attunement Questions
- What connections do I have with irises and transcendence?
- Where else in the green world or in my life do I observe transcendence?
- What does transcendence feel like?
- How can I describe this energetic attribute of transcendence in words or pictures?
- Where does this correspondence of transcendence resonate most strongly in or around my body or in my life?

Daily Integration Questions
- In what ways is the world reflecting irises or transcendence back to me?
- What nuances and shades of meaning do I notice about irises and transcendence?

Evening Reflection Questions
- Where and how did I experience irises or transcendence today?
- How did I embrace this attribute of transcendence today?
- What wisdom does the iris's correspondence of transcendence bring to my life?

Week 23

Strawberry and Heart-Centeredness

Fragaria spp.

The arrival of strawberries in the spring is heralded with festivals, strawberry desserts, and other delectables. Strawberries are one of the easiest and best fruits to grow in the home garden. Many of the cultivars grown for market are selected for their size and ability to be easily transported; flavor comes third. If you grow your own strawberries, you can have sweet taste as your first criteria. Popping a freshly picked strawberry into your mouth and experiencing that burst of flavor is a blissful experience that grocery store strawberries cannot match.

Strawberry plants are low to the ground, not usually more than twelve inches high. The fruit is often sheltered under the leaves, so it's a bit of a treasure hunt pushing away leaves to discover the ripe berries. Strawberries spread by sending out long runners that touch the ground and root to create new plants. My strawberries are forever escaping from the beds and starting new plants along the paths and edges. The escapees have allowed me to provide many of my friends with strawberry plants.

Strawberry's correspondence, heart-centeredness, is determined by its shape, that of a tiny heart. Many cultures have recognized the heart as an energetic wisdom center. The fourth chakra and qigong's middle dantian, both energy centers, are in the heart area. Even though Western medicine has viewed the heart as simply a pump, poets and philosophers knew it was more than that. In English, phrases like "follow your heart" and "heart of gold" indicate this awareness. On an intuitive level, it is clear that the heart is intimately connected to emotions, compassion, and empathy.

The fact that strawberries are sometimes hidden under the leaves illustrates another facet of heart energy. We sometimes armor ourselves and hide our hearts so our emotions won't be impacted by the world, but in doing so, we cut ourselves off from others.

Heart-centeredness is about making a choice to lead with empathy and compassion. As you mindfully work with this correspondence for the week, remind yourself to shift to heart-centeredness throughout the day. One way to cultivate this awareness is to imagine you are breathing in and out through the heart center. Intentionally move your awareness from your head to your heart, observing how that changes your perception of the situation.

Morning Attunement Questions

- What connections do I have with strawberries and heart-centeredness?
- Where else in the green world or in my life do I observe heart-centeredness?
- What does this correspondence feel like?
- How can I describe this energetic attribute of heart-centeredness in words or pictures?
- Where does this correspondence of heart-centeredness resonate most strongly in or around my body or in my life?

Daily Integration Questions

- In what ways is the world reflecting strawberries or heart-centeredness back to me?
- What nuances and shades of meaning do I notice about strawberries and heart-centeredness?

Evening Reflection Questions

- Where and how did I experience strawberries or heart-centeredness today?

- How did I embrace heart-centeredness today?

- What wisdom does the strawberry's correspondence of heart-centeredness bring to my life?

Week 24
Flax and Serendipity
Linum usitatissimum

In the fairy tale Rumpelstiltskin, a poor farmer's daughter must spin straw into gold to save her life. With Rumpelstiltskin's help, she pulls it off. This is a neat trick, but it is just fiction. The true story of how flax is turned into fiber is much more fascinating.

Flax is entwined with human history. Woven flax fibers discovered in a cave in the Caucasus Mountains are estimated to be 19,000 to 23,000 years old.[25] Please think about that for a moment. In ancient Egypt, linen (the fabric made from flax) was used to wrap mummies, including King Tut. Linen shawls and wraps were often buried in the tombs. Linen is mentioned in both the Bible and Homer's Odyssey. Flax has been used as fiber for a very long time.

Making fiber from flax is something of a puzzle. There are other plants that more easily suggest fiber; cotton, for example, encases its seeds with fuzzy material. You can see and feel the fuzzy material. It's easy to understand why early humans used cotton for fiber, but what drew them to flax?

Flax is a wispy-stemmed plant with small, vibrant blue flowers and feathery leaves. Looking at the plant, you would not think there is fabric hidden inside somewhere. Yet our ancestors figured this out and used flax for a multitude of applications, including string, rope, flags, and clothing.

---

25. St. Clair, *Golden Thread*, 23.

The process of turning flax into fiber is not a simple one. Plants are first pulled from the ground (not cut) and dried. Once dried, the seed heads are removed and the flax is immersed in water until the stems rot. This takes several weeks. Next, there is another drying process and further combing and sorting to get to the usable fiber, which can then be spun and woven.

It is fascinating to imagine the series of happy coincidences that occurred to ensure the discovery of flax as fiber. Perhaps wild flax was uprooted in a wind storm and then dried out; another wind blew the flax into a shallow pond where the stems began to rot; at just the right time the pond dried up; and the flax lay there until a child began to play with it and began pulling fibers from the material that was left. We'll never really know.

Serendipity, a happy, accidental discovery, is the correspondence for flax. Sometimes serendipity has the mark of fate about it, a feeling that we were absolutely supposed to discover or encounter something. Serendipity is not just about the big events in our lives; there are plenty of small serendipitous events if we are paying attention. The universe opens and we stumble upon a wonderful new book, a quiet hiking path, a musical artist we'd never heard of, or a new person in our lives.

Your personal serendipitous events might not be as momentous as discovering a fiber that clothed humans for thousands of years, but looking for serendipity is another way to tune in to the flow of moments, recognize connections, and be present.

Morning Attunement Questions

- What connections do I have with flax and serendipity?
- Where else in the green world or in my life do I observe serendipity?
- What does this correspondence feel like?
- How can I describe this energetic attribute of serendipity in words or pictures?
- Where does this correspondence of serendipity resonate most strongly in or around my body or in my life?

Daily Integration Questions

- In what ways is the world reflecting flax or serendipity back to me?

- What nuances and shades of meaning do I notice about flax and serendipity?

Evening Reflection Questions

- Where and how did I experience flax and serendipity today?

- How did I embrace the concept of serendipity today?

- What wisdom does flax's correspondence of serendipity bring to my life?

Week 25
Black-Eyed Susan and Justice
Rudbeckia hirta

Black-eyed Susan is a North American perennial wildflower. Native Americans used the plant as a medicinal herb, most notably for treating infections and snake bites.[26] At first glance, a black-eyed Susan, with its dark center and yellow, daisy-like petals, could be confused with the sunflower. It's shorter than the sunflower, and there are other differences as well. The Susan's center is a darker brown and the petals are a bright orangish-yellow, creating a striking contrast. Black-eyed Susans also have a more pronounced rounded cone that pushes up and away from the petals.

Black-eyed Susans usually make their appearance midsummer, often growing wild in clumps along roadsides and in open spaces. The plant's hardiness and beauty make it a popular garden plant as well. They grow easily and are tolerant of a wide range of conditions, including the dry, hot summers here in Denver.

Black-eyed Susan has a history of countering toxins, including snake venom, and it is the perfect symbol for countering a community toxin: injustice. Its hardiness and tolerance for different situations resonates with the idea of justice, its energetic correspondence. If you pass by a field of black-eyed Susans,

---

26. Warmund, "Rudbeckia."

you can almost imagine them confidently standing as a strong, deeply rooted community to support fairness and justice.

Humans seem to have an innate longing for justice. Most people agree that creating a just world is a worthy goal. We attempt to make the world a fairer place with rules, laws, and traditions. It doesn't take much observation to notice that we've not been completely successful. One challenge is that we each perceive justice from our own unique perspective. The difference in colors between a black-eyed Susan's center and petals reminds us that within the same community, there might be strikingly different ideas of what is just and fair. While bringing mindful awareness to the concept, we can step back in an objective way and listen to others' points of view on justice.

When holding the concept of justice in your awareness, you may quickly slide into focusing on injustices. Unfairness abounds on the planet, and there is much work to do, but as a starting point, place your attention on the accomplishments of justice. Pay attention to the wrongs that have been righted. These may be issues in your personal life or in the wider world.

In considering injustices, be aware of your own circle of influence. You can't do everything, but you can usually do *something*. How might you contribute and make a difference? How might you speak up or take a stand in some way?

Millions of people around the planet are working to counterbalance injustice through sharing, cooperation, and challenging the status quo. Take time to acknowledge the work that has been done in the pursuit of justice; this shines a light on the positive and expands your awareness of what is possible.

Morning Attunement Questions

- What connections do I have with black-eyed Susans and justice?
- Where else in the green world or in my life do I observe justice?
- What does this correspondence feel like?
- How can I describe this energetic attribute of justice in words or pictures?
- Where does the correspondence of justice resonate most strongly in or around my body or in my life?

Daily Integration Questions

- In what ways is the world reflecting black-eyed Susans or justice back to me?

- How does energy shift when justice is achieved?

- What nuances and shades of meaning do I notice about black-eyed Susans and justice?

Evening Reflection Questions

- Where and how did I experience black-eyed Susans or justice today?

- How did I embrace justice today?

- What wisdom does the black-eyed Susan's correspondence of justice bring to my life?

Week 26

Lady's Mantle and Solitude

Alchemilla vulgaris

Lady's mantle is a low-growing perennial with large, round-lobed leaves, resembling a cloak (or mantle). The drops of dew that collect on the leaves each morning were once thought to hold magical powers and were used in alchemical potions. Lady's mantle has also been used for a variety of women's health issues, but that is not where the name of the plant originates. In *A Modern Herbal*, Maude Grieve explains the plant was named for the cloak of Mary (mother of Jesus), so the "lady" in the name refers to a specific woman.[27]

When I look at lady's mantle, I imagine the women in Jane Austen novels as they walked along the English moors wrapped in their cloaks. Cloaks and mantles provide protection from the elements, but also a kind of solitude, which is the energetic correspondence for this plant.

Solitude is a different energy than aloneness or loneliness. Solitude is a choice and willingness to spend time with ourselves. When we are constantly focusing outward, it is hard to know who we are and what we want. It may be difficult to make choices that align with our values or even to know what our values are. Solitude enriches our lives by creating a space for the new and original to grow and be nourished. It removes us from the fray so that we can take stock of our lives.

---

27. Grieve, *A Modern Herbal*, vol. II, 463.

Solitude can be a challenge in today's world; I am fairly certain that Jane Austen could walk along the moors in contemplation without running into throngs of other people. In contrast, my morning walk with my dog Luna is noisy and chaotic with cyclists, joggers with baby strollers, other dog owners, people talking on the phone, skateboarders, and clusters of jostling school children. Not only am I surrounded by others, I must be careful that my dog and I don't get run over—and that is just the start of my day. The busy world has a way of encroaching on any planned alone time. Even when you are physically alone, you may have constant intrusions from electronic devices.

If you see the value of solitude, you can be intentional in carving out small amounts of time for yourself. It's also possible to be in the world and not *of* the world, wrapping an imaginary cloak of solitude around yourself as you move through your day.

In contemplating this plant and its correspondence, notice when you allow yourself to be in solitude, if at all. Pay attention to the feeling of solitude and ask yourself if it feels burdensome, boring, nourishing, or something else.

Morning Attunement Questions

- What connections do I have with lady's mantle and solitude?
- Where else in the green world or in my life do I observe solitude?
- What does this correspondence feel like?
- How can I describe this energetic attribute of solitude in words or pictures?
- Where does this correspondence of solitude resonate most strongly in or around my body or in my life?

Daily Integration Questions

- In what ways is the world reflecting lady's mantle or solitude back to me?
- What nuances and shades of meaning do I notice about lady's mantle and solitude?

Evening Reflection Questions

- Where and how did I experience lady's mantle or solitude today?

- How did I embrace solitude today?

- What wisdom does lady's mantle's correspondence of solitude bring to my life?

Week 27

Raspberry and Birth

Rubus idaeus

When I was growing up, our neighbors had a large—though not very well-cared for—raspberry patch. It was a tangled, scratchy mess and difficult to get to many of the berries. Left to their own devices, raspberries will become unwieldy. However, there are some newer varieties of raspberries for the home garden that are tidier and easier to grow. The golden raspberry that grows in my yard does not get overly tall or tangled, and it is a great addition to the grazing garden. The stems of golden raspberries are still a little scratchy, but it is much easier to enjoy the delicious fruit.

In addition to the fruit, the leaves of raspberries can be made into a nutritious tea. The leaves are rich in minerals including iron, calcium, and potassium and high in vitamins B and C. The tea has a long history as an aid to pregnant women in many parts of the world. Drinking raspberry-leaf tea is credited with strengthening and toning the uterus and helping ensure a healthy pregnancy, labor, and birth. During my last pregnancy, I took the advice of drinking raspberry-leaf tea to heart and drank four to six cups a day. For whatever reason, whether it was the raspberry leaves or just good luck, my labor was fast and easy.

Because of this strong connection to pregnancy, birth is the correspondence for this plant. This includes much more than birthing a child. It's the idea of new beginnings and manifestations coming into being when something that didn't exist previously is suddenly revealed. We give birth to new ideas, friendships, creative projects, and habits. Any time a new concept or way of being pops up in the world, it is a kind of birth.

There is a gestation period before birthing that ideally includes nourishing, nurturing, and supporting the process. There will probably be labor involved with any new project; it may not be effortless.

Be attentive to what is being born in your life and the lives of those you love. Look for ways to be a midwife to that process by facilitating and supporting what is being born. While contemplating this correspondence, ask yourself what is being born and how you might provide help.

Morning Attunement Questions

- What connections do I have with raspberries and birth?
- Where else in the green world or in my life do I observe the concept of birth?
- What does this correspondence feel like?
- How can I describe this energetic attribute of birth in words or pictures?
- Where does this correspondence of birth resonate most strongly in or around my body or in my life?

Daily Integration Questions

- In what ways is the world reflecting raspberries or birth back to me?
- What nuances and shades of meaning do I notice about raspberries and birth?

Evening Reflection Questions

- Where and how did I experience raspberries or the concept of birth today?
- How did I embrace this attribute of birth today?
- What wisdom does the raspberry's correspondence of birth bring to my life?

Week 28
Mullein and Gentleness
Verbascum thapsus

The first time a friend saw mullein growing in my yard, she said, "You know that's a weed, right?" Mullein is a medicinal herb that grows in abandoned areas, and, yes, some people think of it as a weed. I hadn't planted this particular mullein plant—the seed had blown into my yard and established itself among the rose bushes, but it was welcome in my yard.

Mullein is a biennial, which means it takes two years for the plant to run through its life cycle. The first year, there is simply a rosette of soft and velvety green leaves. The second year, it sends up a tall flower stalk from the middle of the plant. In late summer, the top of the stalk is covered with a myriad of small, soft, yellow flowers. Mullein hardly qualifies as a weed since it is not invasive and can easily be pulled out if it is growing in the wrong place. It might be thought of as a weed because it grows wild along roadways, but this is because mullein grows easily in hot, dry conditions. I think the plant looks majestic growing in the yard.

Mullein has been used medicinally by Native Americans and Western herbalists. The plant has demulcent properties, which means it is soothing to mucous membranes. The leaves and flowers can be brewed into a tea to relieve coughs and bronchial problems. In the past, smoking the herb was recommended for asthma and coughs. The flowers have also been blended with olive oil to soothe ear infections.

Gentleness is the correspondence for mullein, reflected in its soothing and gentle medicinal properties. We sometimes equate gentleness with weakness, but mullein is a reminder that they are not the same. Mullein can grow four or five feet tall and makes a bold statement in a yard or along the roadside. It is a hardy plant that stands tall, yet it exhibits softness and gentleness.

Gentleness can include patience and tolerance, and there is a strength with both of those words as well. Gentleness can also be a choice grounded in strength and exhibited by thoughtful actions.

When considering this correspondence, be aware of where and how gentleness manifests in your life. Pay attention to whether or not you sometimes confuse gentleness with weakness.

Morning Attunement Questions

- What connections do I have with mullein and gentleness?
- Where else in the green world or in my life do I observe gentleness?
- What does this correspondence feel like?
- How can I describe this energetic attribute of gentleness in words or pictures?
- Where does this correspondence of gentleness resonate most strongly in or around my body or in my life?

Daily Integration Questions

- In what ways is the world reflecting mullein or gentleness back to me?
- What nuances and shades of meaning do I notice about mullein and gentleness?

Evening Reflection Questions

- Where and how did I experience mullein or gentleness today?
- How did I embrace gentleness today?
- What wisdom does mullein's correspondence of gentleness bring to my life?

Sunchokes and Community

Helianthus tuberosus

In late summer, sunchokes create a beautiful display of yellow daisy-like flowers on tall, multi-branched stems. They are sometimes called Jerusalem artichokes because people identified the flavor of the edible root, or tuber, as similar to an artichoke, but the two plants are not related.

The tubers are long, bumpy, and oddly shaped with a mildly sweet flavor. They can be dug up and eaten in the fall and early spring. The tubers also make a great addition to salads and stir-fries, where they can take the place of water chestnuts. They are a good source of B vitamins, potassium, and iron, but moderation is recommended when eating them. The tubers are high in inulin, a substance that can cause gastric distress in some individuals.

The tubers are quick to multiply and will spread out to create a dense community of tubers and flowers. In Pennsylvania, I grew my sunchokes in an old bathtub sunk into the ground and that worked well to contain them. Each year I would harvest a generous amount of tubers and they would quickly regenerate. In my Denver landscape, the sunchokes are in a part of the yard that does not get regular watering. They have proven they are xeric, continuing to spread out without much water or maintenance.

Sunchokes' correspondence is community. They resonate with community in more ways than by simply creating lots of plants. My daughter, who spent many years as a community gardener in Montana, noted that sunchokes are often popular in community garden plots. (They probably escaped from one plot and gardeners embraced them as an easy-to-grow edible.)

Because of their wild nature and ability to grow quickly, sunchokes have supported communities through difficult times. During World War II, French citizens depended on sunchokes as a source of nutrition that kept people and communities alive.[28]

As you hold the concept of community in your awareness this week, first notice the communities in your gardens and green world. Plants support each other in a variety of ways, from sharing nutrients to providing shade or mulch. Next, pay attention to how healthy human communities maintain themselves. We don't have the capability to quickly create new members as sunchokes do, but there are many things we can do to nurture community. As an example, within community gardens, a lot of thought is given to maintaining and growing relationships. There are rules of engagement so everyone understands expected behaviors, and there are opportunities to enrich relationships through potlucks and other events.

Also pay attention to your communities of choice and your communities of happenstance. Communities of choice include your friendship circles and may include your neighborhood or work group. Communities of happenstance are those you've ended up in without planning or intent. These accidental communities may be happy surprises or groups that challenge you in some way. For the first time in human history, we can now participate in virtual communities, gathering with people across the planet in online groups.

As you consider these various communities, notice that they have both benefits and deficits. While mindfully exploring the intricacies of communities, bring the advantages and challenges into conscious awareness. You might want to explore how to navigate the challenges in a positive way and how you can expand on the benefits.

Morning Attunement Questions

- What connections do I have with sunchokes and community?
- Where else in the green world or in my life do I observe community?

---

28. Bloch-Dano, *Vegetables*, 40–41.

- What does community feel like?
- How can I describe this energetic attribute of community in words or pictures?
- Where does this correspondence of community resonate most strongly in or around my body or in my life?

Daily Integration Questions

- In what ways is the world reflecting sunchokes or community back to me?
- What nuances and shades of meaning do I notice about sunchokes and community?

Evening Reflection Questions

- Where and how did I experience sunchokes or community?
- How did I embrace community today?
- What wisdom does the sunchoke's correspondence of community bring to my life?

Week 30
Fennel and Illumination
Foeniculum vulgare

Fennel offers up three licorice-tasting parts—the bulb, the leaves, and the seeds. The delicate, feathery leaves are beautiful in the garden and release a fragrance when brushed against. My favorite is bronze fennel, which, as the name implies, has a distinctive color. When harvesting the leaves and bulb, gardeners keep the plant trimmed and may miss the beauty of the plant flowering and going to seed. An unchecked fennel plant may reach four to five feet, throwing out many branches and an explosion of flower heads that resemble a starburst fireworks display.

Fennel is a perennial, but it doesn't always survive my Denver winters. It grows easily from seed; allowing the seeds to fall from the plant will usually result in a host of fennel volunteers next season.

In Greek mythology, Prometheus gifted humans with fire by sneaking some coals into a fennel stalk. In the story, it changed the course of human history. Fire not only provided warmth and the ability to cook food, it provided a psychic illumination that transformed humans into more intelligent and inventive beings. The myth indicates that humans were not just without light and heat, they were in the dark about what they could do and be. With its starburst flowers and its mythic role in lighting up our minds, fennel has the energetic correspondence of illumination.

Illumination, of course, has multiple meanings. Illumination can simply be bringing light to an area. While holding an awareness of this week's word, be conscious of your ability as a human being to produce light at will. For much of human history, our movements were governed by when the sun was shining. Now, we bring light to a room with the flick of a switch.

Illumination also has a more metaphysical meaning. In the Greek myth, Prometheus is credited with quickening the intelligence and growth of humans. He provided a doorway to understanding and possible enlightenment. Most of us can think of a time when we felt in the dark about something, big or small, and then were provided with information that illuminated our understanding—there is a noticeable shift in energy when that occurs.

In considering illumination, it's good to remember that Prometheus did not bring humans a blazing torch. It was a few smoldering coals hidden away in the hollow of the fennel stalk. Those tiny sparks illuminated the whole world. As you hold this correspondence in mindful awareness, you might notice areas of your life that could benefit from illumination. There may be coals and embers hidden away that need to be fanned to spark increased light. Consider how to cultivate a starburst of beautiful fireworks and illumination in your life.

Morning Attunement Questions

- What connections do I have with fennel and illumination?
- Where else in the green world or in my life do I observe illumination?
- What does this correspondence feel like?
- How can I describe this energetic attribute of illumination in words or pictures?
- Where does this correspondence of illumination resonate most strongly in or around my body or in my life?

Daily Integration Questions

- In what ways is the world reflecting fennel or illumination back to me?
- What nuances and shades of meaning do I notice about fennel and illumination?

Evening Reflection Questions

- Where and how did I experience fennel or illumination?

- How did I embrace illumination today?

- What wisdom does fennel's correspondence of illumination bring to my life?

Week 31
Daylily and Impermanence
Hemerocallis spp.

The long, flat leaves of daylily plants rise up from a central core and appear almost fernlike. In midsummer, flower stalks develop, followed by funnel-shaped flowers. The yellow and orange flowers are common along roadways, where they grow wild. Most flowers only last for a day, thus the name daylily. Although each flower lasts only a day, the plant continues to produce blooms for many weeks in mid-to-late summer.

Daylily flowers are edible. (Remember that daylilies are a different plant than Asiatic lilies; Asiatic lilies are not edible.) They have a light, sweet flavor and look beautiful in salads. Since they make their appearance for only a day, don't feel guilty harvesting them—more will come. The flower buds are also edible and can be steamed or included in stir-fries, although I dislike using the flower buds because it means I will miss seeing the flowers.

Impermanence is the energetic correspondence for daylilies because of the flower's brief existence. Impermanence is a matter of perspective. You could point to the daylily's short existence and call it impermanent, but you could also make a case that each moment of our lives is impermanent as it shifts and changes into the next. Each flower or vegetable in our gardens is a unique expression that manifests and then dies away. Within our own bodies, cells are changing and dying each moment—some live only a few days. We might see friends or family on a daily basis, but each time we connect with them is its own unique event and has an impermanent nature to it, if we are paying attention.

Giant sequoias and bristlecone pines live thousands of years. To them, the human life span might seem impermanent. Focusing on this reality may generate sadness, but it can also generate deep appreciation and wonder for the moment-by-moment flow of our lives. Each moment is precious, and we should embrace it as is. Tuning in to the impermanent and transitory nature of reality helps us discern what is important and what is not.

Morning Attunement Questions

- What connections do I have with daylilies and the correspondence of impermanence?
- Where else in the green world or in my life do I observe the concept of impermanence?
- What does this correspondence feel like?
- How can I describe this energetic attribute of impermanence in words or pictures?
- Where does this correspondence of impermanence resonate most strongly in or around my body or in my life?

Daily Integration Questions

- In what ways is the world reflecting daylilies or the correspondence of impermanence back to me?
- What nuances and shades of meaning do I notice about daylilies and impermanence?

Evening Reflection Questions

- Where and how did I experience daylilies and impermanence?
- How did I embrace the concept of impermanence?
- What wisdom does the daylily's correspondence of impermanence bring to my life?

Week 32

Collards and Dependability

Brassica oleracea var. viridis

In late summer, collard leaves spread out from their center stalk in multiple spiraling layers. The large elongated, oval leaves form a rosette, looking like a huge jade-green flower. Collards are well-behaved in the garden. They can get tall, but they don't get unwieldy or invade their neighbor's space. Collards are a reliable leafy green that provide lots of healthy eating in a range of temperatures. They don't bolt in the heat like some other greens, and cold actually improves their flavor.

Collards have not been promoted the way kale has, yet collards have many of the same nutrients and functions in recipes. They are a good source of calcium, as well as vitamins C and K. Young leaves can be included in salads and smoothies. Larger leaves can be steamed and used to wrap rice and vegetables before baking. Collards are great in soups and stews, but my favorite method is to chop and steam them with lots of garlic and a touch of balsamic vinegar.

Once collards are in the ground and mulched, I don't have to fuss with them. They are hardy and dependable. The plants will take a light frost and keep on producing. I often have greens until winter solstice. They are the essence of dependability, which is their energetic correspondence.

A key feature of dependability in others is that you don't have to think about them a lot. In contrast, if something is undependable, you often spend a lot of mental energy on it. If you have an undependable vehicle, it might be on your mind all morning as you get ready for work. *Is it going to start this morning? Will I get to my destination?* If you have an undependable friend, you can't fully trust that they will do the things they tell you they will do, whether it is walking your dog or attending a party. You might love an undependable person, but their unreliability will always be in the back of your mind as you make plans.

Dependability means that someone or something is solid and trustworthy. There is ease and safety in interacting with dependable entities. They don't take up a lot of your energy, allowing you to focus on other matters. The downside is that it is easy to let dependable entities slide off your radar into forgetfulness, and you might not always acknowledge their value.

When exploring this correspondence, begin by considering your own dependability and if it is a trait that others would use to describe you. Is it a value you personally embrace? Push that awareness into the world around you and consider the people, places, and other entities that feel dependable. As you bring this concept into your awareness, be aware of the dependable entities you count on and send them thanks.

Morning Attunement Questions

- What connections do I have with collards and dependability?
- Where else in the green world or in my life do I observe the concept of dependability?
- What does this correspondence feel like?
- How can I describe this energetic attribute of dependability in words or pictures?
- Where does this correspondence of dependability resonate most strongly in or around my body or in my life?

Daily Integration Questions

- In what ways is the world reflecting collards or dependability back to me?
- What nuances and shades of meaning do I notice about collards and dependability?

Evening Reflection Questions

- Where and how did I experience collards or dependability today?
- How did I embrace dependability?
- What wisdom does the collard's correspondence of dependability bring to my life?

Week 33
Pole Beans and Exploration
Phaseolus vulgaris

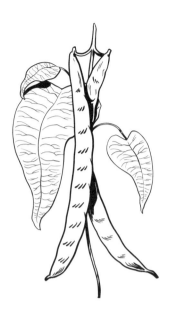

In the fairy tale "Jack and the Beanstalk," Jack trades the family cow for a bag of magic beans. His mother is so angry by his apparent naivete that she throws the beans out the window. The next morning the beans have grown into a sturdy stalk that reaches beyond the clouds. Jack climbs up the stalk to discover a giant's kingdom, and Jack's fortune is forever changed.

A small part of this fairy tale is grounded in truth. Pole beans are viny plants that can grow to ten feet or more depending on the variety, and they grow quickly and easily. However, they don't grow overnight, and they can't grow upward without support. As their name suggests, they need a pole, a trellis, or other support to reach upward.

While all beans are high in protein, pole beans produce more when compared to their cousins, the bush beans (also known as green beans). This makes them a great choice for small gardens. It is fun to watch the tendrils of young pole beans as they reach out in various directions until they find something to latch on to. They explore their environment, turning one way and then another, until they find what they need. Like Jack, the plants embody a correspondence of exploration.

Small children are expert explorers as they try to learn about the world. As we get older, we may feel as if we have our world mapped out and there is no need for further exploration. Like Jack's mom, we might feel we don't need to know about anything new and different. Often, our map of the world doesn't allow for the possibility of magic beans or anything that will dramatically alter our current understanding, yet the world is constantly shifting and changing.

Searching your physical environment is only one dimension of this correspondence. It also includes your whole being—physical, emotional, and spiritual. When you mindfully attune to the correspondence of exploration, consider the edges of your personal maps and the discoveries you might make if you push beyond those edges. Be attentive to your comfort or discomfort with this idea.

Mindfully exploring your world might include truly listening to others when they are explaining their view of the world. It might include investigating where your values and beliefs originated. Like pole beans, it is only by reaching out and exploring that you find what you need. Consider whether exploration feels comfortable, scary, exciting, or something else. Discoveries await you when you push beyond the edges.

Morning Attunement Questions

- What connections do I have with pole beans and exploration?
- Where else in the green world or in my life do I observe pole beans or exploration?
- What does this correspondence feel like?
- How can I describe this energetic attribute of exploration in words or pictures?
- Where does this correspondence of exploration resonate most strongly in or around my body or in my life?

Daily Integration Questions

- In what ways is the world reflecting pole beans or exploration back to me?
- What nuances and shades of meaning do I notice about pole beans and exploration?

Evening Reflection Questions

- Where and how did I experience pole beans or exploration today?
- How did I embrace exploration today?
- What wisdom does the pole bean's correspondence of exploration bring to my life?

Week 34
Yarrow and Healing
Achillea millefolium

Yarrow is a common wildflower found along hiking trails, roadsides, and in empty lots, but it is also popular in perennial gardens. The leaves are fernlike, soft, and feathery. The flower heads, composed of many tiny flowers, are white, off-white, or pink in the wild. More brilliant reds and pinks are now available for gardeners.

Yarrow has a long history and strong resonance with healing. The plant is astringent and antiseptic, so it can help stop the flow of blood and reduce infection. This made it a popular herb on battlefields though the ages. Some of its common names include soldier's woundwort and knight's milfoil. *Achillea*, the first part of the plant's Latin name, is often attributed to Achilles, who is said to have used yarrow to heal his troops during the Trojan War 3,000 years ago.

The correspondence for yarrow is healing. This includes any type of healing. On a personal level, it is emotional and physical recovery. In a bigger arena, it includes community and planetary healing.

Healing can only begin when we stop the damage. Yarrow has the ability to stop the flow of blood, allowing the first restorative steps to be taken. This is a process, not an instantaneous event. There is always a turning point with healing. When we are healing from a wound, grief, or injustice, we may not recognize that turning point until we are past it. It can be challenging to be patient as we recuperate.

When tuning in to healing or the need for healing, be mindful that bodies and systems are more fragile as they begin the recuperative process. Intentionally support this process in yourself and others by being aware of this fragility.

Healing is a response to woundedness. As you consider this energy, first focus on the woundedness itself. However, it is important to not get stuck there; trace the transition back to healing.

Morning Attunement Questions

- What connections do I have with yarrow and healing?
- Where else in the green world or in my life do I observe healing?
- What does this correspondence feel like?
- How can I describe this energetic attribute of healing in words or pictures?
- Where does this correspondence of healing resonate most strongly in or around my body or in my life?

Daily Integration Questions

- In what ways is the world reflecting yarrow or healing back to me?
- What nuances and shades of meaning do I notice about yarrow and healing?

Evening Reflection Questions

- Where and how did I experience yarrow or healing today?
- How did I embrace healing today?
- What wisdom does yarrow's correspondence of healing bring to my life?

Week 35
Beets and Balance
Beta vulgaris

Roasted beets are one of my go-to dishes, especially in the fall and winter. Beets are hearty and warming. Roasting them highlights their sweet and earthy flavor. They can be cooked and added to dips and even snuck into brownies to create a healthier treat. Uncooked beets can also be grated and included in salads and smoothies. They are a good source of B vitamins, potassium, and magnesium.

Beets are an easy garden crop. They don't need much room, and any gardener will be richly rewarded with a hearty food that stores well after being harvested. Beets come in a range of colors, from deep purples to golden and even striped, so you can plant something different from what might be found at the market.

There is more to beets than the root. The entire plant is edible. Leafy beet greens and stems are another nutritious food. The leaves and stems can be steamed or used in place of any other green like spinach. Young leaves can be added to salads and smoothies. They are a good source of vitamins C and A.

Beets are a root crop and a leafy green. They are of the earth and of the air. The roots are substantial and solid, but the leafy greens are light and airy. Their correspondence is balance. Balance in our lives is often achieved by feeling rooted, yet comfortable with reaching out and pushing the boundaries.

The world and its inhabitants routinely swing in and out of balance. Earth travels around the sun, arcing out to its farthest distance at winter and summer solstice, the extremes of disequilibrium. Then it arcs back, reaching equilibrium at autumn and spring equinox, when the hours of day and night are equal.

As children, some of our earliest accomplishments are about mastering physical balance as we learned to stand and walk. We had to concentrate as we were practicing this skill, but once learned, it became automatic for most of us. We move through our day making constant unconscious adjustments to stay in equilibrium.

Balance has different facets. There is balance, or need for balance, in the world at large. Our personal sense of equilibrium is affected by the state of the world or our perception of it. In maintaining personal balance, we often navigate between multiple divergent points without giving them much consideration. This includes movement and stillness, solitude and engagement with the world, and work and family. There may be a gentle shifting back and forth as with a rocking chair, or you may experience a more dramatic shift that can make you feel unstable. It is usually only when you reach a state of serious disequilibrium that balance—or the lack thereof—comes to your attention.

As you focus on balance, notice this dance of equilibrium that you are constantly engaged in, bringing it to your conscious awareness. Notice balance in the world around you and the practices that help you and the world remain in balance.

Morning Attunement Questions

- What connections do I have with beets and balance?
- Where else in the green world do I observe balance?
- What does balance feel like?
- How can I describe this energetic attribute of balance in words or pictures?
- Where does this correspondence of balance resonate most strongly in or around my body or in my life?

Daily Integration Questions

- In what ways is the world reflecting beets or balance back to me?
- Where are beets or balance manifesting in my life?
- What nuances and shades of meaning do I notice about beets and balance?

Evening Reflection Questions

- Where and how did I experience beets or balance today?
- How did I embrace balance today?
- What wisdom does the beet's energy of balance bring to my life?

Week 36
Comfrey and Strength
Symphytum officinale

Comfrey is a beautiful addition to a perennial bed. It dies down in the winter, but quickly emerges in the spring with the appearance of long arrow-shaped, hairy leaves. By early summer, the plant is tall and stately, with delicate, blue bell-shaped flowers.

Comfrey has been recognized for thousands of years as a healing herb. In the past, the roots and leaves were used internally and externally to speed the healing of wounds, sprains, and broken bones. *Symphytum* comes from the Greek word *symphis*, which means the growing together of bones. Other common names for the plant include knitbone and knitback, indicating this resonance with healing and strengthening bones.

Comfrey contains allantoin, a protein that promotes healing. External application of comfrey with salves, oils, and poultices has proven its efficacy in reducing pain and speeding healing, but herbalists no longer recommend taking comfrey internally.

Because of its relationship to healing bruises and broken bones, comfrey's correspondence is strength. In addition to strengthening bones, comfrey lends strength to the garden. Comfrey is known as a dynamic accumulator, a plant that reaches deep into the soil to pull calcium, magnesium, potassium, and other minerals up into its leaves and stems. The plant can be cut and used as mulch or added to the compost to help strengthen the entire garden. In my Denver garden, I get three crops of comfrey every summer.

Comfrey's contribution to the garden does not end there. Its deep roots help break up clay and hard soil. It's also a great companion plant in orchards because the bell-shaped flowers attract a multitude of bees. Comfrey easily propagates from root cuttings, and I've been able share the wealth of comfrey with many friends.

We often think of strength as a personal attribute—plants or individuals can be strong during challenging weather or situations. However, comfrey's correspondence of strength is one that is shared with others. It creates a stronger and healthier garden and community. As you mindfully focus on strength, be aware of this expanded meaning.

Morning Attunement Questions

- What connections do I have with comfrey and strength?
- Where else in the green world or in my life do I observe strength?
- What does this correspondence feel like?
- How can I describe this energetic attribute of strength in words or pictures?
- Where does this correspondence of strength resonate most strongly in or around my body or in my life?

Daily Integration Questions

- In what ways is the world reflecting comfrey or strength back to me?
- What nuances and shades of meaning do I notice about comfrey and strength?

Evening Reflection Questions

- Where and how did I experience comfrey or strength today?
- How did I embrace strength today?
- What wisdom does comfrey's correspondence of strength bring to my life?

Week 37
Fungi and Connectedness

Fungi

Scientists classify fungi in their own kingdom, distinct from plants and animals. They are included here because their presence in the garden and the green world is instrumental in creating healthy environments and soil. They are crucial to the decomposition of organic waste, which adds nutrients to the soil. In addition to creating healthy soils, some varieties have strong healing properties for humans and other mammals. Mushrooms like reishi, maitake, and shiitake have been used in traditional Chinese and Ayurvedic medicine for thousands of years. Categorized as adaptogens, fungi help our bodies cope with stress and remain balanced.

We are usually only aware of fungi when a mushroom, the fruiting part of the organism, pops up in our garden or compost pile. Supporting that mushroom is a vast network of underground and unseen threads called mycelia. Fungi don't produce their own food as plants do. Instead, they connect with plants to share water and nutrients in exchange for plant sugars.

However, their connection with the green world is more than a one-on-one exchange of nutrients. Mycelia can spread out in soil for miles and are able to connect plants to other plants, facilitating nutrient sharing and chemical communication. All of this happens below ground and out of sight. When we think about it, this symbiotic relationship looks more like one big organism than separate entities.

Fungi are the essence of connectedness, their energetic correspondence. We probably have connections within our family and community, and like fungi, we might share resources and information. That's a starting point, but the correspondence of connectedness pushes beyond family and community. Connectedness is the experience of being part of a larger whole. It's a kinship with other living organisms.

As you contemplate connectedness, consider your connections to other people, your communities, and to other organisms on the planet. Often these connections are hidden like the mycelia. Shining the light of awareness on the many ways you are connected to the natural world and to other people highlights the reality of this correspondence. Our natural state is one of connectedness.

Morning Attunement Questions

- What connections do I have with fungi and connectedness?
- Where else in the green world or in my life do I observe connectedness?
- What does this correspondence feel like?
- How can I describe this energetic attribute of connectedness in words or pictures?
- Where does this correspondence of connectedness resonate most strongly in or around my body or in my life?

Daily Integration Questions

- In what ways is the world reflecting fungi or connectedness back to me?
- What nuances and shades of meaning do I notice about fungi or connectedness?

Evening Reflection Questions

- Where and how did I experience fungi or connectedness today?
- How did I embrace connectedness today?
- What wisdom does fungi's correspondence of connectedness bring to my life?

Week 38

Mums and Transition

Chrysanthemum spp.

There are always a few days each summer when the garden is peaking and it feels like summer could go on forever; vegetables are producing abundantly, flowers all look happy ... Then there is a subtle shift and the peak is over. Flowers are changing to seed heads. Where plants looked vibrant a few days before, some now look tired. In my yard, yellow chickadees show up to begin eating sunflower seeds and squirrels are increasingly on patrol to steal ripening apples and tomatoes.

That's when chrysanthemums, or mums, burst onto the scene. In colors of rust, copper, deep orange and yellow, and muted lavender and mauve, they herald the coming of fall. My favorites are the ones that look like many-legged spiders, but they can also take the shape of puffy pompoms or daisies. The common element is the mounded nature of the plants. A profusion of flowers pops out of the mound of greenery.

Mums are hardy perennials and will emerge from a light snow or frost to keep blooming, often until Thanksgiving. In Erie County, Pennsylvania, where I grew up, we'd visit a farm each year that had acres of chrysanthemums. Sometimes my family visited because we needed to replace a plant that didn't make it through the winter, but often it was just to wander through the beautiful sea of mums on a fall day.

Chrysanthemums have the energetic correspondence of transition. Mums arrive just as the days are getting shorter and nights are getting cooler. Their beautiful display eases us into fall. Transitions are times of shifting and changing, but they are not abrupt changes like a hailstorm. We have time to prepare for change and adjust to the new order of things.

It's true that most of life is a transition from one state to another; however, some transitions require more attention and adjustment from us. Chrysanthemums remind us that transitions can be beautiful. When embracing this energetic concept for the week, tune in to the important transitions in your life. Sometimes the important transitions are the most subtle. Pay attention to what is shifting and changing to another state of being. It might be a season in the garden or a season in your life. If you have children in the house, there are transitions around kindergarten, middle school, and college. Then there is the transition of watching your children have children. Transitions might mean shifts in relationships, careers, or living spaces. Transitions are a flowing wave of energy. Like a wave, they are made up of countless moving parts. Sometimes you are riding the wave, and other times the wave has pulled you under a little (or a lot).

Morning Attunement Questions

- What connections do I have with mums and transition?
- Where else in the green world or in my life do I observe transition?
- What does this correspondence feel like?
- How can I describe this energetic attribute of transition in words or pictures?
- Where does this correspondence of transition resonate most strongly in or around my body or in my life?

Daily Integration Questions

- In what ways is the world reflecting mums or transition back to me?
- What nuances and shades of meaning do I notice about mums and transition?

Evening Reflection Questions

- Where and how did I experience mums or transition today?

- How did I embrace transition today?

- What wisdom does the mum's correspondence of transition bring to my life?

Week 39
Pumpkin and Abundance
Cucurbita pepo

My grandchildren christened my pumpkin patch "pumpkinpalooza," an apt description for the bold, overflowing plants. In mid-to-late summer, the pumpkin vines become a moving mass of leaves with large orange flowers that resemble cornucopia baskets. Bees don't hover around the flowers, but instead land and disappear down into them. The vines are resilient—I once accidentally broke a stem and then wrapped it with duct tape. It mended itself and kept right on growing.

Many people think of pumpkins as good for jack-o'-lanterns and Thanksgiving pies. Pumpkins are much more versatile. They are a kind of winter squash and so, as a start, they can be used in any recipe calling for winter squash. One thing to take note of, however, is that jack-o'-lantern pumpkins are bred for color and size, so they don't have the best flavor or texture. Make sure you have a pumpkin bred for eating if you are making a meal.

Pumpkins, like all winter squash, have tougher skins than their summer squash siblings. This means they can be stored for winter eating. I often have garden pumpkins last for five or six months. The importance of this might be lost on us because we can easily go to a grocery store and buy food, but it wasn't that long ago that putting food away for the winter was extremely important and might be the difference between life and death.

Pumpkins and winter squash are among the easiest foods to store for the winter. There is no canning, drying, or freezing involved. Once the pumpkin is cut from the vine, it's cured by leaving it outside so the outer skin and stem dry out. Then it should be put in a cool, dry place. That's it! Although it is not a necessity for most of us to store food for the winter, it is satisfying to create a meal from our garden when there is snow falling outside.

Abundance is the correspondence for pumpkin, recognizing its wild growth, productivity, and storage capabilities. The word abundance usually refers to monetary abundance, but it is so much more than that. Abundance is a feeling that there is an endless supply of something good, a cup running over.

Abundance can show up in many ways in your life—big and small—when you are paying attention. You might have an abundance of energy, friends, or good books to read. In the garden, we hope for an abundance of pollinators and an abundant harvest. On the Colorado plains, after spring rains, we have an abundance of wildflowers. As you consider this correspondence, also be aware of what the earth abundantly provides for us.

Morning Attunement Questions

- What connections do I have with pumpkins and abundance?
- Where else in the green world or in my life do I observe abundance?
- What does this correspondence feel like?
- How can I describe this energetic attribute of abundance in words or pictures?
- Where does this correspondence of abundance resonate most strongly in or around my body or in my life?

Daily Integration Questions

- In what ways is the world reflecting pumpkins or abundance back to me?
- What nuances and shades of meaning do I notice about pumpkins and abundance?

Evening Reflection Questions

- Where and how did I experience pumpkins and abundance today?
- How did I embrace abundance today?
- What wisdom does the pumpkin's correspondence of abundance bring to my life?

Week 40
Tomato and Shape-Shifting
Solanum lycopersicum

Tomato plants are incredibly easy and rewarding plants to grow. They produce abundantly and have thousands of varieties with a range of colors from dark purple to light yellow. In gardens with mild winters, tomatoes are perennials. Where I live, they won't make it through the first frost without protection and so are treated as annuals, replanted each year.

Tomatoes are shape-shifters, which is their energetic correspondence. The part we eat is botanically a fruit, but nutritionists classify tomatoes as vegetables because they are not overly sweet and show up most often in dinners. Tomatoes do, however, shape-shift into great sweets and desserts. I've made green tomato pie, tomato jam, and tomato tarts. They also shape-shift easily in their vegetable role, appearing raw in salads and gazpacho and cooked in dishes from lasagna to masala.

Tomatoes are ubiquitous in so many dishes that it is hard to imagine there was a time when people were afraid to eat them. Only a few hundred years ago, tomatoes were thought to be poisonous.[29] They have shape-shifted in the minds of humans from poisonous to nutritious. Tomatoes (along with eggplants and potatoes) are members of the nightshade family, which includes deadly nightshade or belladonna. As the name implies, deadly nightshade is toxic to humans. Tomato flowers resemble deadly nightshade flowers, so it would have

---

29. Bloch-Dano, *Vegetables*, 70.

been a logical leap to think the tomato fruit was as poisonous as its distant cousin. Thankfully for pizza and ketchup lovers, we no longer believe that.

Shape-shifting is something we all do, but not always consciously. We have different modes of behavior with friends, family, coworkers, children, and strangers. Our shape-shifting is a little different than tomatoes' in that it is a protective mechanism we engage in; we reveal only certain parts of ourselves. Knowing how to act in different settings is an important skill to master early on, but it can become automatic and unconscious. Hopefully, our values remain consistent across these different characters we inhabit.

Being attentive to when you are shape-shifting is a mindfulness practice. Pay attention to your shifts in character and engagement, noticing when and why you are doing it and allowing others to do that as well. Let go of any judgment about shape-shifting, but investigate how the shape-shifting is serving you. Perhaps, in some settings, you've outgrown the need to shape-shift. You might find that you can meld some of your different personas, but you also might discover your different roles are still exercising a strong protective value.

Bringing intentional awareness to the process can illuminate how and why it happens. There may be an energy you pick up from different friends, locations, or clothes. The mindfulness aspect of shape-shifting is noticing that you are doing it and being intentional with your actions and words.

Morning Attunement Questions

- What connections do I have with tomatoes and shape-shifting?
- Where else in the green world or in my life do I observe shape-shifting?
- What does this correspondence feel like?
- How can I describe this energetic attribute of shape-shifting in words or pictures?
- Where does this correspondence of shape-shifting resonate most strongly in or around my body or in my life?

Daily Integration Questions

- In what ways is the world reflecting tomatoes or shape-shifting back to me?
- What nuances and shades of meaning do I notice about tomatoes and shape-shifting?

Evening Reflection Questions

- Where and how did I experience tomatoes or shape-shifting today?
- How did I embrace awareness of this attribute of shape-shifting today?
- What wisdom does the tomato's correspondence of shape-shifting bring to my life?

Week 41
Sage and Wisdom
Salvia officinalis

Sage is a shrubby plant with grey-green leaves and delicate purple-lipped flowers. It is drought tolerant and looks great in a xeric landscape. Sage grows happily here in Denver and, when flowering, it is always abuzz with bees. Sage is popular as a culinary seasoning. With a mild eucalyptus-like flavor, it perks up vegetable dishes and salads. Leaves can be brewed for tea as a remedy for sore throats. In ancient times, drinking sage tea was thought to increase brain power and longevity.

Sage has a strong resonance with wisdom, its correspondence. The word sage means knowledgeable, as in having "sage advice." The word also refers to a mentor, elder, or wise person. Sage's reputation for contributing to longevity is also related to wisdom. If you live a long life, you have more opportunities for wisdom to develop.

Wisdom is more than knowledge or brain power. It can be helped by reading and study, but it is not simply a collection of facts. Wisdom is a combination of lived experience enriched by contemplation.

The green world has its own wisdom for maintaining balance and life. One example is that plants can recognize predators and secrete chemicals to make themselves less tasty. When gardening, we can seek out knowledge of how the natural world functions so that we can co-create with it, rather than approaching it with poisons and insensitivity.

Our bodies have a wordless internal wisdom, born from experience, about what is good for us. Paying attention to that wisdom might help us avert illness and accidents. Feelings of being off-balance, headaches, and pain could be communications from our body's wisdom.

Intuition is another kind of wordless wisdom that can be developed by paying attention to our comfort and discomfort with situations and people. Rather than disregarding feelings, intentionally explore what you are sensing.

If wisdom comes from experience plus careful attention, it is something that can be cultivated. Consciously review what you've experienced to glean insight. Seek out wisdom from the green world and from others and intentionally apply it in your life.

Morning Attunement Questions

- What connections do I have with sage and wisdom?
- Where else in the green world or in my life do I observe wisdom?
- What does this correspondence feel like?
- How can I describe this energetic attribute of wisdom in words or pictures?
- Where does this correspondence of wisdom resonate most strongly in or around my body or in my life?

Daily Integration Questions

- In what ways is the world reflecting sage or wisdom back to me?
- What nuances and shades of meaning do I notice about sage and wisdom?

Evening Reflection Questions

- Where and how did I experience sage or wisdom today?
- How did I embrace wisdom today?
- What does sage's correspondence of wisdom bring to my life?

Week 42
Rosemary and Ancestors
Rosmarinus officinalis

Many people are familiar with rosemary as a culinary herb. It is great on roasted potatoes and other vegetables. It is also often part of herbal blends because a little goes a long way. It has a strong, piney flavor that can easily be overpowering.

Rosemary is a perennial evergreen shrub with small, blue, fragrant flowers. It has a long history as a plant of remembrance. It has been used at funerals, weddings, and other ceremonies with the purpose of remembering our connection to the past.

The correspondence for rosemary is ancestors. This isn't about filling out genealogy charts, although you might choose to research your ancestors in that way. This is about cultivating an awareness that who and what you are in this moment is a unique manifestation of countless ancestors, stretching back through the ages.

Tuning in to your ancestors in a mindful way might include gratitude that you are here, a curious investigation into all the ways they have influenced you, or simply realizing the commonality of human experience.

We all carry our ancestors with us in various ways. Our genes, culture, and language shape us, often without our conscious participation. We may feel like our modern life is very different than someone who lived 100 or even 1,000 years ago, yet there are some commonalities of experience. Love, loss, and grief are universal. For example, I remember that surge of love when holding each of my children in my arms and simultaneously realizing my mother had this same experience. I have this connection across time with my mother, grandmothers, and great-grandmothers back through the ages.

Throughout history, there were many twists and turns that made up your genetic and energetic mix. One of those twists can be seen in my family's lineage. During World War II, my father served on two different ships that were sunk. Many of his friends and shipmates died, but he was rescued each time. I'm here because of a twist of fate, for which I am grateful.

You don't exist in a bubble. There are innumerable human ancestors that led us to today, whether they are in your direct lineage or not. Be grateful to your ancestors who began gardening, discovered the healing power of herbs, created fiber from plants, created language, told stories, made each other laugh, and did so much more. Acknowledge every positive invention, helpful discovery, philosophy of kindness, and hope that helps nurture our world. Tuning in to that unbroken connection to your ancestors is the correspondence of rosemary.

Morning Attunement Questions

- What connections do I have with rosemary and ancestors?
- Where else in the green world or in my life do I observe ancestors?
- What does this correspondence feel like?
- How can I describe this energetic attribute of ancestors in words or pictures?
- Where does this correspondence of ancestors resonate most strongly in or around my body or in my life?

Daily Integration Questions

- In what ways is the world reflecting rosemary or ancestors back to me?
- What nuances and shades of meaning do I notice about rosemary and the ancestors?

Evening Reflection Questions

- Where and how did I experience rosemary or ancestors today?
- How did I embrace the energy of ancestors today?
- What wisdom does rosemary's correspondence of ancestors bring to my life?

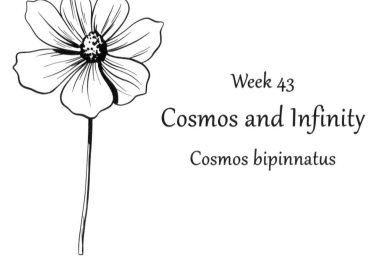

Cosmos and Infinity

Cosmos bipinnatus

In midsummer, my backyard is a sea of pink and purple cosmos flowers. The feathery leaves and abundant blossoms sway and ripple with each small breeze. Cosmos self-seed easily, so the previous year's seeds pop up in unintended places. I don't have the heart to pull them out. Before I know it, they are copiously flowering all over the yard with bees and butterflies hovering nearby.

Cosmos have a neat trick of surviving our spring hailstorms, of which there are many. The hail seems to slide through the wispy leaves, leaving the plants undamaged. They are also drought resistant, another good trait here in Denver. They continue to flower and look great when other flowers are drooping in the heat. In autumn, the seed heads resemble little starbursts, an association with the heavens and the cosmos.

My granddaughter has declared that I have too many cosmos in the yard, something we disagree on. We do agree that the flowers appear to be infinite, which is the correspondence for this plant. Cosmos flowers are named from the Greek word *kosmos*, which "refers to an equal presence of order and beauty."[30] It was first used by the matemtician Pythagorus to describe the universe. Cosmos flowers have a strong resonance with infinity and the boundless nature of the universe because of their name and their behavior.

---

30. JRank Science & Philosophy, "Pythagoreanism."

As you hold this concept of infinity in your awareness, you might notice there are things you describe as infinite because they feel that way, whether they are truly boundless or not. For example, I might label love, creativity, children's energy, and the cosmos in my yard as infinite. You might also be challenged by home or work situations that feel endless and unmanageable. It may be helpful to remind yourself that they are not.

True boundlessness is the nature of the universe. Consider how the idea of infinity touches you. Having no limits may feel like freedom, but it can feel immobilizing as well, or somewhere in between.

One way to get a sense of true infinity is to head out to the garden at night and look up at the stars. What does it mean to be on a small planet traveling in infinite space? Can you hold that question in your being for the week, examining your place in the scheme of things?

Morning Attunement Questions

- What connections do I have with cosmos and infinity?
- Where else in the green world or in my life do I observe infinity?
- What does this correspondence feel like?
- How can I describe this energetic attribute of infinity in words or pictures?
- Where does this correspondence of infinity resonate most strongly in or around my body or in my life?

Daily Integration Questions

- In what ways is the world reflecting cosmos or infinity back to me?
- What nuances and shades of meaning do I notice about cosmos and infinity?

Evening Reflection Questions

- Where and how did I experience cosmos or infinity today?
- How did I embrace this correspondence of infinity today?
- What wisdom does cosmos's correspondence of infinity bring to my life?

Week 44
Hops and Power
Humulus lupulus

My grandchild has named my sprawling hops vine Audrey, after the plant in *Little Shop of Horrors*. My Audrey has not eaten anyone yet, but she has drawn blood. She grows prolifically, so sometimes the fingerlike, scratchy tendrils catch us by surprise as we are walking by.

The plant is a perennial but disappears completely in winter. In early spring, the shoots push up from the ground in a powerful and dramatic way, almost shouting, "I'm here!" I can leave for work on a spring morning with no trace of hops and when I return later in the day, the shoots have pushed up through the ground six inches. Once up, the vines grow quickly, wrapping themselves around the trellis and anything else within reach. In a few weeks, they have completely sheltered the patio. The thick hops vine, with its maple-like leaves, provides welcome relief from the intense Denver sun.

The flowers make their appearance in midsummer. They resemble papery, light-green pine cones with a strong and heady fragrance. Most people know that hops flowers are used to brew beer, and this has been true since the ninth century. Hops flowers are also a powerful relaxation and sleep aid when used in tea or dried and stuffed in small pillows.

From its powerful appearance in the spring to its ability to intoxicate and create sleepiness, the plant exudes power, which is the plant's correspondence.

Power is a tricky attribute. We know from experience that it can be wielded unwisely and unfairly. It can cause harm even when that is not the intention, like when Audrey unintentionally scratches us. However, power by itself is not a bad thing.

Power is often subtle. You may chalk it up to just the way the world works and not question it. Sometimes you might hide from power, pretending you don't see it or it doesn't exist. You should also honestly consider if you ignore abuses of power when they don't affect you personally. Paying attention to power, your own and that of others, is a first step to using power in a positive way. You may not be able to completely change a power dynamic, but when you examine it, you might see opportunities for shifting the energy in a positive way. That can only happen with attentiveness.

If you have personal power, whether because of good fortune or effort, mindfully acknowledge it and work to share that power with others. Note when others are using power in a destructive way and, if possible, take action.

Mindfully focusing on this concept allows you to examine how you embrace your personal power and the ways you might push the envelope to use it in positive ways.

Morning Attunement Questions

- What connections do I have with hops and power?
- Where else in the green world or in my life do I observe power?
- What does this correspondence feel like?
- How can I describe this energetic attribute of power in words or pictures?
- Where does this correspondence of power resonate most strongly in or around my body or in my life?

Daily Integration Questions

- In what ways is the world reflecting hops or power back to me?
- What nuances and shades of meaning do I notice about hops and power?

Evening Reflection Questions

- Where and how did I experience hops and power today?

- How did I embrace this attribute of power?

- What wisdom does hops' correspondence of power bring to my life?

Week 45
Violet and Hidden Treasure
Viola odorata

I first discovered violets as a young child while walking with my mother in what was left of a grove of trees behind our house. That grove was scheduled to be cut down for new housing, so my mother rescued the violets and moved them to her rose garden.

Violets are easy to miss when walking in the woods or in the garden. Low to the ground and only flowering in the early spring, they don't call out to you as other plants might. There are no flashy flowers or strong fragrances to make you stop and pay attention. They prefer partial shade and are happy living in the shadow of taller plants. It's easy to simply walk by them. In some ways, noticing violets at all requires you to be attentive and mindful. If you can find them, violet flowers and leaves are edible (though not the seeds) and make a lovely addition to spring salads.

Paying attention will help you discover hidden treasures that are on the periphery of your vision. Hidden treasures include strengths in yourself or those around you that you haven't appreciated. The concept also includes the blessings you overlook or take for granted.

Violets' heart-shaped leaves remind us of another aspect of this correspondence: the treasures we keep hidden in our hearts. They may be cherished memories, people you love, or people you've lost. They are the things you keep close to your heart and only share with your inner circle, or perhaps no one at all. Even though you keep them hidden, they influence you in many ways. Tuning in to those treasures and acknowledging them in an intentional way allows you to explore whether you want to continue to keep them hidden from view. The correspondence of violets incorporates both aspects of hidden treasure— the treasures you've missed by not paying attention and the treasures you've purposefully hidden.

As you work with this correspondence for the week, intentionally seek out hidden treasures within you and around you. This might include the kind actions of family members or coworkers who you ignore on a regular basis. It might include your own strengths or hidden talents that you don't fully embrace. Play an intentional game with yourself and seek out hidden treasures, especially in difficult situations.

Morning Attunement Questions

- What connections do I have with violets or hidden treasure?
- Where else in the green world or in my life do I observe hidden treasure?
- What does this correspondence feel like?
- How can I describe this energetic attribute of hidden treasure?
- Where does this correspondence of hidden treasure resonate most strongly in or around my body or in my life?

Daily Integration Questions

- In what ways is the world reflecting violets or hidden treasure back to me?
- What nuances and shades of meaning do I notice about violets and hidden treasure?

Evening Reflection Questions

- Where and how did I experience violets and hidden treasure today?
- How did I embrace the concept of hidden treasure today?
- What wisdom does the violet's correspondence of hidden treasure bring to my life?

Week 46
Basil and Harmony
Ocimum basilicum

Basil has many varieties, and like fine wines, there are nuances with flavor and fragrance. Dominant flavors may include clove, anise, and lavender, but it is sometimes hard to fully describe the blend of basil's flavor in any one plant.

There are sizes of basil for every garden and pot. I like large-leafed basil for making pesto and its ease of harvesting. Basil likes hot weather and will produce all summer if you keep clipping the leaves and remove any flowers that pop up. Planting it near a walkway enables you to release its delightful fragrance as you brush by. It grows easily in the garden and on kitchen windowsills, so with some planning, you can have fresh basil year-round.

Basil has been part of Mediterranean cuisine for hundreds of years. It can be dried and frozen, but it is most flavorful when used fresh. It is the key ingredient in pesto, a sauce made by blending fresh basil with garlic, olive oil, and pine nuts. Most of us use food processors for creating pesto, but it was originally made with a mortar and pestle, grinding the ingredients together by hand until they became a harmonious blend.

Basil is a culinary star in other fresh dishes like gazpacho, bruschetta, and salads, but it has also been employed as a healing herb to aid digestion and soothe anxiety. A specific variety called Tulsi, or holy basil, is sacred in India, where it is recognized as an herbal adaptogen.[31] Adaptogens create harmony in the body by enhancing the ability of internal organs to work optimally. Holy basil is also credited with harmonizing the chakras, energy centers within our bodies that contribute to our health and well-being, when functioning well.

Harmony is the correspondence for basil, reflecting its role in blending and complementing flavors in the kitchen and as a healing plant that reduces stress. In the musical realm, harmony results from individual sounds coming together to create a new blended sound. The result is greater than the individual parts. Harmony evolves out of diversity.

In bringing intentional awareness to harmony this week, first notice harmony in the green world. What diverse plants come together and contribute to a unique whole, especially in open spaces? When preparing meals, notice how distinct tastes blend to create harmony. Even within the same plant, there may be a blend of flavors.

In your communities, pay attention to how and when harmony is occurring. We sometimes assume that peace can only occur when everyone reaches like-minded agreement about ideas. However, diverse sounds can blend into one harmonious and better whole. Harmony means you can sing your own song and blend it with those around you who are singing their own unique songs. Working toward and recognizing harmony is an intentional process.

There are some kinds of jazz that at first sound disharmonious, but in careful listening, the harmony arises. You may have situations at work or in your families where a more jazzlike harmony is manifesting. Holding harmony in your awareness, step back and listen for the blended sound.

Morning Attunement Questions

- What connections do I have with basil or harmony?
- Where else in the green world or in my life do I observe harmony?
- What does this correspondence feel like?
- How can I describe this energetic attribute of harmony in words or pictures?
- Where does this correspondence of harmony resonate most strongly in or around my body or in my life?

_____

31. Winston and Maimes, *Adaptogens*, 167–71.

Daily Integration Questions

- In what ways is the world reflecting basil or harmony back to me?
- What nuances and shades of meaning do I notice about basil and harmony?

Evening Reflection Questions

- Where and how did I experience basil or harmony today?
- How did I embrace this attribute of harmony today?
- What wisdom does basil's correspondence of harmony bring to my life?

Week 47
Burdock and Purpose
Arctium lappa

If you or your dog have come home with burrs on your clothes or fur, you've probably had an accidental encounter with a burdock plant. Burdock is a biennial, wild food and medicinal herb. It is considered a weed by some. All parts of the plant are edible. Burdock is rich in vitamins and minerals and is recognized as a healing plant in both Western and Chinese herbal medicine. It tones and nourishes internal organs and helps them function in an optimal way.

The plant has large elephant-ear leaves that resemble rhubarb. Flower stalks emerge from the leaves and develop sticky purple flowers by midsummer. The flowers morph into seedpods with tiny barbed prongs that easily stick to anything that touches them. My grandchildren have been fascinated by the stickiness of the seed heads. One year, they tried experimenting with different liquids to see if soaking the seedpods would soften the barbs and stop the plants from sticking. They tried vinegar, milk, dish detergent, and hot water. Nothing worked.

George de Mestral, a Swiss engineer, was also fascinated by the barbed seed heads. He began studying the plant in 1941, with a goal of replicating the seed head's sticky mechanism. It took him many years, but he was finally successful in developing the product we all know as VELCRO.[32]

---

32. Velcro, "About VELCRO Brand."

Purpose is the correspondence for burdock, as it exemplifies a single-minded purpose in getting its seeds out into the world. Admittedly, scattering seeds is the goal of most plants, but burdock fulfills its purpose with an ingenious seed-scattering system. Purpose also has a strong resonance with burdock's herbal healing role, as it supports each organ of the body to fulfill its purpose.

When mindfully focusing on this concept, cultivate an awareness of where purpose is showing up in your life and in the world. You can begin in the garden. You might wonder what the purpose of tomato hornworms and other garden predators are, other than destroying plants. Of course, from the hornworm's perspective, its purpose is to find food and stay alive.

Intentionally shifting your focus to consider purpose from the perspective of the people and situations you find challenging can be part of the exploration this week. Shine an intentional light on your own purpose in being, in working, and in relating to others. There may be discoveries around behaviors and habits that you haven't recognized as being successful and others that have outlived their original purpose.

Morning Attunement Questions

- What connections do I have with burdock or purpose?
- Where else in the green world or in my life do I observe the energy of purpose?
- What does this correspondence feel like?
- How can I describe this energetic attribute of purpose in words or pictures?
- Where does this correspondence of purpose resonate most strongly in or around my body or in my life?

Daily Integration Questions

- In what ways is the world reflecting burdock or purpose back to me?
- What nuances and shades of meaning do I notice about burdock and purpose?

Evening Reflection Questions

- Where and how did I experience burdock or purpose today?

- How did I embrace the correspondence of purpose today?

- What wisdom does burdock's correspondence of purpose bring to my life?

Week 48
Sunflower and Guardians

Helianthus annuus

Sunflowers are one of the most recognizable flowers. They tower over other garden plants, reaching ten or eleven feet. The flowers resemble the sun, or at least a child's drawing of the sun. They look like big happy faces. Horticulturists have bred smaller varieties, but I like the old-fashioned towering plants.

All parts of the sunflower are edible, although not always tasty. The flower petals are a little bland and have a bitter aftertaste; they are not your best choice for edible flowers. The flower buds can be steamed and taste a lot like artichokes, but I hate harvesting the buds as it means one less flower to enjoy. The seeds are nutritious and tasty, but you will have to battle the birds and squirrels to get them. It may be best to give up and just enjoy the fun of watching birds and squirrels hanging in various positions from the seed heads while trying to get their fill.

Sunflowers line my front walkway and my back fence. They stand like guardians of the green space, sending out a bright, positive, protecting energy. The sunflower guardians also help protect my mood. When I open my windows or doors in the morning, there they are, standing tall with their happy faces. Their sunny yellow faces shine a light on the space around them.

Guardians are protectors and caretakers, and they show up in our lives in many forms. Firstly, we are our own guardians in protecting our time, values, and personal space. Like sunflowers, we can attempt to do all of this with a happy face. When being mindful of guardians, we may notice ways that others have shown up for us that we have taken for granted. Guardians appear in our communities as elders and teachers who remind us of community values and our purpose in life.

There are less visible sorts of guardians as well. The power in books, music, philosophies, and spiritual practices can act as guardians. They may stand between you and negative feelings, or they might help you interpret difficult situations so you can filter them in slowly. As you mindfully consider this correspondence, notice all the different types of guardians in your life. You may want to reach out and give thanks to them. Also take note of how you are a guardian for yourself and others.

Morning Attunement Questions

- What connections do I have with sunflowers and guardians?
- Where else in the green world or in my life do I observe guardians?
- What does this correspondence feel like?
- How can I describe this energetic attribute of guardians in words or pictures?
- Where does the correspondence of guardians resonate most strongly in or around my body or in my life?

Daily Integration Questions

- In what ways is the world reflecting sunflowers or guardians back to me?
- What nuances and shades of meaning do I notice about sunflowers and guardians?

Evening Reflection Questions

- Where and how did I experience sunflowers or guardians today?
- How did I embrace the energy of guardians today?
- What wisdom does the sunflower's correspondence of guardians bring to my life?

Week 49
Butterfly Weed and Essentiality

Asclepias tuberosa

Butterfly weed is a wildflower in the milkweed family. It stands three to four feet tall with orange tiny flowers clustered together. In the fall the seedpods release the cottony seeds that milkweed plants are known for. Bees, hummingbirds, and butterflies love it.

Butterfly weed is also known as pleurisy root. It was first used by Native Americans, who introduced it to the Europeans. The plant was a remedy for pleurisy and other respiratory conditions that made breathing difficult. Because of its effectiveness, it was included in the United States Pharmacopeia in the early 1900s.[33]

Butterfly weed joined my garden family in the last few years after I learned that even adding one plant to your home garden can help the monarch caterpillars. It's part of my butterfly garden bed, along with bee balm and *Echinacea*.

Butterfly weed, like all members of the milkweed family, is crucial to the survival of monarch butterflies. Monarchs are in danger because urbanization and the increased use of herbicides have reduced the availability of their food. Monarch butterflies can feed on many different flowers, but the caterpillars *must* have milkweed to survive. Without caterpillars, there cannot be butterflies.

---

33. Grieve, *A Modern Herbal*, vol II, 647.

Any milkweed species will meet the food requirements of monarch butterflies; however, it is important to choose a variety recommended for your specific area. The tropical varieties available at some garden centers will flower longer, and this encourages the butterflies to not migrate, which can result in their death.[34] Butterfly weed meets the requirements for most of the United States, but you can confirm this by entering your zip code at the website www .monarchwatch.org.

Historically, the plant played a critical role in supporting breathing, an essential part of life. It also plays a critical role in the life cycle of monarchs. Because of these relationships, essentiality is the energetic correspondence of butterfly weed. When you turn your mindful awareness to this correspondence, consider what is critical and nonnegotiable for your existence.

In our consumer culture, it is easy to confuse what is essential (our needs) with what we simply want. As a parent and grandparent, I've often heard children say they need something when it is actually a desire; they confuse desperately wanting something with needing it. Of course, it is always easier to notice these behaviors in others. If I am truthful, I know I also can get lost in the call of bright and shiny new things, especially in garden catalogs. This isn't about judging people who want things that are shiny and new; it's about bringing awareness to the difference between want and need by evaluating what is essential in our lives.

As you go about your day, be mindful of what is essential to your well-being. Certainly, food, air, water, and shelter are essential to your physical well-being. Start by recognizing their importance. Remember, though, that life is not only about physical well-being. Be intentional in noticing what is indispensable to your emotional and mental well-being as well—friendship, community, spirituality, music, books, and solitude might fit into this category.

Morning Attunement Questions

- What connections do I have with butterfly weed and essentiality?
- Where else in the green world or in my life do I observe essentiality?
- What does this correspondence feel like?
- How can I describe this energetic attribute of essentiality?

---

34. Save Our Monarchs, "Monarchs Need Milkweed."

- Where does this correspondence of essentiality resonate most strongly in or around my body or in my life?

Daily Integration Questions

- In what ways is the world reflecting butterfly weed or essentiality back to me?
- What nuances and shades of meaning do I notice about butterfly weed and essentiality?

Evening Reflection Questions

- Where and how did I experience butterfly weed or essentiality today?
- How did I embrace essentiality today?
- What wisdom does butterfly weed's correspondence of essentiality bring to my life?

Calendula and Creativity
Calendula officinalis

Calendula flowers are sometimes called pot marigold, but this is a different plant than the marigold we looked at in Week 5. Calendula flowers have graced my gardens for as long as I can remember. The orange and yellow many-petaled flowers resemble small suns. Once they start to bloom, the flowers continue all summer with their beautiful display.

With its bright yellow and orange flowers, calendula has a strong resonance with creativity, the correspondence for this plant. Calendula flowers can be used in all sorts of creative ways. The flowers are edible and look lovely in salads and other dishes. Because the petals keep their color when dried, they can be stored to brighten a winter meal or liven up frosting on cupcakes.

Calendula is a healing plant, good for cuts, bruises, burns, and skincare of all kinds. The flowers are so prolific that it is easy to gather some without ruining the beauty of the plants. I harvest the flowers every year to create healing oils and salves, as well as to include them in homemade soaps. My grandchildren and I have blended them into our paper-making experiments to create flecks of orange and yellow throughout the paper. The flowers can also be used to dye wool.

Creativity belongs to all of us. We may sometimes limit our thinking by only associating creativity with artists, but we all engage in creative processes whenever we produce something new in the world. This doesn't have to be a big creation—making dinner, arranging a bouquet, or painting a room are all creative endeavors. If you have your own garden, you can stop and appreciate the act of nurturing it into existence. It represents the flow of your creative energy made manifest.

When it comes to creativity, you might be inspired by necessity or just have the urge to make something original or interesting. Whatever the reason, humans' creativity is visible everywhere. With every creative process, there is a moment where an idea you have held in your mind makes its way into three-dimensional reality. Paying mindful attention to the creative process and manifestation allows you to tap into that flow.

Morning Attunement Questions

- What connections do I have with calendula and creativity?
- Where else in the green world or in my life do I observe creativity?
- What does this correspondence feel like?
- How can I describe this energetic attribute of creativity in words or pictures?
- Where does this correspondence of creativity resonate most strongly in or around my body or in my life?

Daily Integration Questions

- In what ways is the world reflecting calendula or creativity back to me?
- What nuances and shades of meaning do I notice about calendula and creativity?

Evening Reflection Questions

- Where and how did I experience calendula or creativity today?
- How did I embrace creativity today?
- What wisdom does calendula's correspondence of creativity bring to my life?

Week 51
Eggplant and Mystery
Solanum melongena

Elongated, round fruit hangs gracefully from the branches of the eggplant plant. The color is usually shiny dark purple, but eggplants can also be white and lavender. They love the heat and are perennials when grown in subtropical areas. In most zones in North America, they are grown as an annual, as they will not survive the first frost.

Like the tomato, eggplant is part of the nightshade family, and, at various times and places around the world, people assumed the plant was poisonous. However, in the Mediterranean, eggplant has been part of culinary traditions for hundreds of years in dishes like baba ghanoush and ratatouille. The spongy texture makes them interesting to work with in the kitchen, as they absorb both oil and flavors easily. If you are a cook, you may know there is controversy about salting eggplant before cooking. I grew up in a household where eggplant slices were salted and left on a plate for an hour before cooking. (The salt is supposed to tenderize and pull out bitterness.) I've often skipped this step without consequences, making it a bit of a mystery as to why this practice exists.

Mystery is the correspondence of eggplant, and it resonates with that energy for reasons beyond salt. With its deep purple color, the color of higher chakras, eggplants symbolize mystery and spiritual quests. Their unusual shape and shiny skin also hint at mystery. The egg shape represents the unknown;

we know there is new life inside, yet we can't see it or know exactly what will develop.

When contemplating this correspondence, you can cast a wide net by recognizing the mysteries that happen every day, both big and small. Some mysteries in our lives are simply fun puzzles to work out, if we care enough to investigate. I have an ongoing garden mystery: I ponder why squirrels like to dig up my plants and leave peanuts in their place. Your mysteries might revolve around why other people do things you can't make sense of, or why you sometimes do things that are not in your own best interest.

At its deepest level, life is a mystery. Theories abound as to what and why we are here, and we may believe one thing or another, but there is a part that is unknowable. The future is also a mystery. No matter what amount of planning you do, there will always be an element of the unknown. Finding a way to accept and even welcome the unknown may be the key to contentment. Cultivate an attitude of curiosity and amusement as you investigate the mysteries in your life. This week's correspondence invites you to be mindfully aware of the mysteries that surround you, finding ways to embrace them as they are.

Morning Attunement Questions

- What connections do I have with eggplants and mystery?
- Where else in the green world or in my life do I observe mystery?
- What does this correspondence feel like?
- How can I describe this energetic attribute of mystery in words or pictures?
- Where does this correspondence of mystery resonate most strongly in or around my body or in my life?

Daily Integration Questions

- In what ways is the world reflecting eggplants or mystery back to me?
- What nuances and shades of meaning do I notice about eggplants and mystery?

Evening Reflection Questions

- Where and how did I experience eggplants or mystery today?

- How did I embrace mystery today?

- What wisdom does the eggplant's correspondence of mystery bring to my life?

Week 52

Snapdragon and Joy

Antirrhinum majus

Snapdragons are beautiful but tidy plants, a perfect addition to a summer garden. The multitude of flowers grow along a one-to-two foot stalk and come in a range of brilliant colors.

I have a distinct memory of the day I discovered snapdragons' magic ability to transform into a talking puppet. A childhood friend and I were playing near a neighborhood garden. She reached over, picked a snapdragon flower, and began to make it talk. The oblong, boxy-shaped flowers resemble a dragon's head. Gently squeezing the sides of the flower makes the "dragon" open and close its mouth. I remember this moment with joy and amazement. At six years old, I'd never seen a flower-puppet before.

Joy may be easier to access as a child when most of the world is new to us. It is also a matter of perspective. It can be a mindful practice to cultivate joy, the energetic correspondence of snapdragons. Children have fresh eyes for the world. We all had those eyes once, even if we don't remember. The world is made new each moment.

You can cultivate this awareness by looking at the world through childlike eyes, allowing yourself to be delighted and dazzled by the simple things. It might take a little more effort than when you were a child, but that's the intentional and mindful part. Direct your attention to appreciating the interesting, quirky, and beautiful, because the world has an abundance of those things.

There is a note taped to my back door that says, "Invoke joy." I see it every day when I leave the house. It's a reminder for me to adjust my focus, so I head out into the world with an orientation toward finding joy.

Tuning in to joy is not about ignoring your personal challenges or the challenges on the planet. You may have worries about yourself or a loved one. Natural disasters and other tragedies might take your breath away at times, but in life there is a balance of light and dark. In the midst of challenging situations, you can usually discover a space of joy if you look with intention. Cultivating joy is a way to hold a light in the darkness.

Morning Attunement Questions

- What connections do I have with snapdragons and joy?
- Where else in the green world or in my life do I observe joy?
- What does this correspondence feel like?
- How can I describe this energetic attribute of joy in words or pictures?
- Where does this correspondence of joy resonate most strongly in or around my body or in my life?

Daily Integration Questions

- In what ways is the world reflecting snapdragons or joy back to me?
- What nuances and shades of meaning do I notice about snapdragons and joy?

Evening Reflection Questions

- Where and how did I experience snapdragons or joy today?
- How did I embrace joy today?
- What wisdom does the snapdragon's energy of joy bring to my life?

CONCLUSION

When choosing the order of the correspondences in part 2, I purposefully chose dandelions and resilience first, and I wanted to end the fifty-two-week practice with snapdragons and joy. Starting with resilience and ending with joy could be a roadmap for any quest, whether we are journeying through the year or a challenging time in our lives.

If working with plant correspondences resonates for you, you can repeatedly explore the practices in part 2. You can also branch out by being present to the correspondences revealing themselves through the green world in your own garden. Alternatively, you can begin with an attribute you'd like to work with; patience or passion, for example. Then, intentionally explore the green world to discover plants that resonate with that energy. Plant correspondences are all around us. They can anchor our awareness. They provide a framework for understanding the world, one that is both helpful and poetic.

Focusing on one plant and one attribute at a time allows you to hone your mindfulness skills. When you embrace this practice, you will more clearly see the interconnectedness of the world. Synchronicities will bubble up into your awareness. The interconnection has always been there—mindfulness reveals it.

Moving Forward with Remembrance

During my first meditation retreat in my early twenties, the facilitators continuously encouraged us to "wake up." The three-day retreat involved instruction and practice with sitting and walking meditation. While it helped me focus my attention and learn to step back from my constantly bubbling thoughts, I felt confused and frustrated. I didn't understand what "waking up" meant. I was trying very hard to get there, but I realize now that I was approaching the practice in a disembodied way, only from my head.

Mindfulness doesn't happen in our heads. It is a holistic awareness of who we are. It can be helped along by an intellectual understanding, but often our minds get in the way as we try to think ourselves into awakening. Our consciousness operates through our bodies, and our bodies are interconnected with green, flowing energy. When practicing mindfulness, we don't want to leave our bodies behind.

Gardens provide a beautiful place of engagement and a portal to awareness. When you are paying attention to the green world, you can transcend the usual limited sense of reality to remember the extraordinariness or your being. We live on a small rock in infinite space protected by an enveloping atmosphere. Within that atmosphere, our lives are made possible by plants and other organisms working together.

Like walking different garden paths, practicing mindfulness can take many directions. In part 1 of this book, we explored a range of green-world activities, from simply focusing to longer, deeper meditations. In part 2, we worked with a specific technique by mindfully holding one plant and correspondence in our awareness for a week. The activities in this book are a small contribution to the millions of ways we can refocus, wake up, and remember who we are—sentient beings experiencing the flow of energy on an interconnected planet. I hope that in some small way, this book has made the waking up and remembering easier for you.

BIBLIOGRAPHY

Bergner, Paul. *The Healing Power of Echinacea and Goldenseal and Other Immune System Herbs.* Rocklin, CA: Prima Publishing, 1997.

Bergner, Paul. *The Healing Power of Garlic.* Rocklin, CA: Prima Publishing, 1996.

Bloch-Dano, Evelyne. *Vegetables: A Biography.* Translated by Teresa Lavender Fagan. Chicago: University of Chicago Press, 2012.

Carroll, Lewis. *The Annotated Alice: 150th Anniversary Deluxe Edition.* Edited by Martin Gardner. New York: W. W. Norton, 2015.

Cole, John N. *Amaranth: From the Past for the Future.* Emmaus, PA: Rodale Press, 1979.

Crocker, Pat. *The Herbalist's Kitchen: Cooking and Healing with Herbs.* New York: Sterling Epicure, 2018.

d'Aulaire, Ingri, and Edgar Parin d'Aulaire. *D'Aulaire's Book of Greek Myths.* New York: Doubleday, 1962.

DeBaggio, Thomas, and Susan Belsinger. *Basil: An Herb Lover's Guide.* Loveland, CO: Interweave Press, 1996.

The Findhorn Community. *The Findhorn Garden: Pioneering a New Vision of Man and Nature in Cooperation.* New York: HarperCollins, 1976.

Gladstar, Rosemary. *Herbal Healing for Women: Simple Home Remedies for Women of All Ages.* New York: Fireside, 1993.

Gregg, Susan. *The Complete Illustrated Encyclopedia of Magical Plants, Revised: A Practical Guide to Creating Healing, Protection, and Prosperity using Plants, Herbs, and Flowers.* Beverly, MA: Fair Winds Press, 2013.

Grieve, Mrs. M., *A Modern Herbal.* 2 vols. 1931. Reprint, New York: Dover Publications, 1971.

Jones, Pamela. *Just Weeds: History, Myths, and Uses.* Shelburne, VT: Chapters Publishing Ltd., 1994.

JRank Science & Philosophy. "Pythagoreanism." Accessed September 18, 2020. https://science
.jrank.org/pages/10928/Pythagoreanism-Number-Cosmos-Harmony.html.

Korzybski, Alfred. *Selections from Science and Sanity*. Fort Worth, TX: Institute of General
Semantics, 2010.

Kowalchik, Claire, and William H. Hylton, eds. *Rodale's Illustrated Encyclopedia of Herbs*.
Emmaus, PA: Rodale Press, 1987.

Li, Qing. *Forest Bathing: How Trees Can Help You Find Health and Happiness*. New York: Viking, 2018.

Lomas, Tim. "Where Does the Word 'Mindfulness' Come From?" *Psychology Today*, March 16,
2016. https://www.psychologytoday.com/intl/blog/mindfulness-wellbeing/201603/where
-does-the-word-mindfulness-come.

McCraty, Rollin. *The Energetic Heart, Bioelectromagnetic Interactions Within and Between People*.
Boulder Creek, CA: HeartMath Institute, 2013.

McGrath, Mike. *Mike McGrath's Book of Compost*. New York: Sterling, 2006.

Miyazaki, Yoshifumi. *Shinrin Yoku: The Japanese Art of Forest Bathing*. Portland, OR: Timber
Press, 2018.

Potter, Jennifer. *Seven Flowers: And How They Shaped Our World*. New York: Overlook Press, 2014.

Robbins, Jim. "Ecopsychology: How Immersion in Nature Benefits Your Health." *Yale Environment 360*, January 9, 2020. https://e360.yale.edu/features/ecopsychology-how-immer
sion-in-nature-benefits-your-health.

Save Our Monarchs. "Monarchs Need Milkweed." Accessed October 30, 2019. https://www
.saveourmonarchs.org/why-milkweed.html.

St. Clair, Kassia. *The Golden Thread: How Fabric Changed History*. London: John Murray Press, 2018.

Warmund, Michele. "Rudbeckia." University of Missouri. March 1, 2008. https://ipm.missouri
.edu/MEG/2008/3/Rudbeckia/.

Winston, David, and Steven Maimes. *Adaptogens: Herbs for Strength, Stamina, and Stress Relief*.
Rochester, VT: Healing Arts Press, 2007.

Velcro. "About VELCRO Brand." About Us. https://www.velcro.com/about-us/our-brand/.

RECOMMENDED READING

Gladstar, Rosemary. *Rosemary Gladstar's Medicinal Herbs: A Beginner's Guide: 33 Healing Herbs to Know, Grow, and Use.* North Adams, MA: Storey Publishing, 2012.

Hemenway, Toby. *Gaia's Garden, A Guide to Home-Scale Permaculture.* White River Junction, VT: Chelsea Green Publishing, 2009.

Haskell, David George. *The Forest Unseen: A Year's Watch in Nature.* New York: Penguin Books, 2013.

Hoffmann, David. *The Herbal Handbook: A User's Guide to Medical Herbalism.* Rochester, VT: Healing Arts Press, 1998.

Jahnke, Roger, and the Institute of Integral Qigong and Tai Chi. IIQTC (website). www .instituteofintegralqigongandtaichi.org.

Jahnke, Roger. *The Healing Promise of Qi: Creating Extraordinary Wellness Through Qigong and Tai Chi.* New York: McGraw-Hill, 2002.

Kabat-Zinn, Jon. *Wherever You Go, There You Are: Mindfulness Meditation in Everyday Life.* New York: Hachette Books, 1994.

Kimmerer, Robin Wall. *Braiding Sweetgrass: Indigenous Wisdom, Scientific Knowledge, and the Teachings of Plants.* Minneapolis, MN: Milkweed Editions, 2013.

Kornfield, Jack. *A Lamp in the Darkness: Illuminating the Path Through Difficult Times.* Boulder, CO: Sounds True, 2014.

Martin, Deborah L. *Rodale's Basic Organic Gardening: A Beginner's Guide to Starting a Healthy Garden.* New York: Rodale Inc., 2014.

Starhawk. *The Spiral Dance: A Rebirth of the Ancient Religion of the Great Goddess.* New York: HarperCollins, 1999.

Toensmeier, Eric. *Paradise Lot: Two Plant Geeks, One-Tenth of an Acre, and the Making of an Edible Garden Oasis in the City.* White River Junction, VT: Chelsea Green Publishing, 2013.

INDEX

To Write to the Author

If you wish to contact the author or would like more information about this book, please write to the author in care of Llewellyn Worldwide Ltd. and we will forward your request. Both the author and publisher appreciate hearing from you and learning of your enjoyment of this book and how it has helped you. Llewellyn Worldwide Ltd. cannot guarantee that every letter written to the author can be answered, but all will be forwarded. Please write to:

Joann Calabrese
⅍ Llewellyn Worldwide
2143 Wooddale Drive
Woodbury, MN 55125-2989
Please enclose a self-addressed stamped envelope for reply,
or $1.00 to cover costs. If outside the U.S.A., enclose
an international postal reply coupon.

Many of Llewellyn's authors have websites with additional information and resources. For more information, please visit our website at http://www.llewellyn.com.